# YOU DON'T NEED TO BE A VEGETARIAN TO EAT LIKE ONE.

Jenny Rosenstrach, creator of the beloved blog *Dinner: A Love Story*, knew that she wanted to eat better for health reasons and for the planet but didn't want to miss the meat that she loves. But why does it have to be all or nothing? She figured that she could eat vegetarian during the week and save meaty splurges for the weekend. *The Weekday Vegetarians* shows readers how Jenny got her family on board with a weekday plant-based mentality and lays out a plan for home cooks to follow, one filled with brilliant and bold meat-free meals.

Curious cooks will find more than 100 recipes (organized by meal type) for comforting, family-friendly foods like Pizza Salad with White Beans, Cauliflower Cutlets with Romesco Sauce, and Roasted Butternut Squash and Black Bean Tacos. Jenny also offers key flavor hits that will make any tray of roasted vegetables or bowl of garlicky beans irresistible—great things to make and throw on your next meal, such as spiced Crispy Chickpeas (who needs croutons?), Hand-Torn Croutons (you need croutons!), and a sweet chile sauce that makes everything look good and taste amazing. *The Weekday Vegetarians* is loaded with practical tips, techniques, and food for thought, and Jenny is your sage guide to getting more meat-free meals into your weekly rotation.

Who knows? Maybe you'll learn what Jenny's family learned: Eating less meat is an addictive lifestyle and philosophy that is likely to take over on the weekends, too!

# the WEEKDAY
## VEGETARIANS

FROM THE
NEW YORK TIMES
BESTSELLING AUTHOR OF
DINNER: A LOVE STORY
**Jenny
Rosenstrach**

# the WEEKDAY VEGETARIANS

PHOTOGRAPHS BY
CHRISTINE HAN

CLARKSON POTTER/
PUBLISHERS
NEW YORK

Copyright © 2021 by Jenny Rosenstrach
Photographs copyright © 2021 by Christine Han

Published by Clarkson Potter/Publishers, an imprint of Random House,
a division of Penguin Random House LLC, New York.
clarksonpotter.com

CLARKSON POTTER is a trademark and POTTER with colophon
is a registered trademark of Penguin Random House LLC.

Some recipes originally appeared on the author's blog,
*Dinner: A Love Story.*

Library of Congress Cataloging-in-Publication Data
Names: Rosenstrach, Jenny, author. | Han, Christine, photographer. Title: The
weekday vegetarians / Jenny Rosenstrach ; photography by Christine Han.
Description: First edition. | New York : Clarkson Potter, [2021] | Includes index.
| Identifiers: LCCN 2021004529 (print) | LCCN 2021004530 (ebook) | ISBN
9780593138748 | ISBN 9780593138755 (ebook). Subjects: LCSH: Vegetarian
cooking. | Vegan cooking. | LCGFT: Cookbooks. Classification: LCC TX837
.R8258 2021 (print) | LCC TX837 (ebook) | DDC 641.5/6362—dc23. LC record
available at https://lccn.loc.gov/2021004529. LC ebook record available at
https://lccn.loc.gov/2021004530.

ISBN 978-0-593-13874-8
Ebook ISBN 978-0-593-13875-5

Photographer: Christine Han
Food Stylist: Olivia Mack McCool
Interior Illustrations: Vitek Graphic
Editor: Raquel Pelzel
Design and hand-lettering: Laura Palese
Production Editor: Patricia Shaw
Production Manager: Kim Tyner
Composition: Merri Ann Morrell and Hannah Hunt
Copy Editor: Kathy Brock
Indexer: Thérèse Shere

Printed in China

10 9 8 7 6 5 4 3 2 1

First Edition

To the next generation:
Abby, Aidan, Alison, Amanda, Luca,
Nathan, Owen, Phoebe, and Sophia

# Contents

# introduction

## WHY NOW?

On a sunny morning a few Octobers ago, I was crossing Atlantic Avenue in Brooklyn on my way to work, when a thought landed in my head as if delivered by lightning bolt: *We need to stop eating so much meat.* The realization was so strong I felt the immediate need to text Andy, my husband, who was on his way to work, too.

**ME:** Should we become vegetarians?

I had no idea how he'd respond. Andy's idea of a perfect dinner has always been an old family recipe for breaded, vinegary pork chops, followed closely by Marcella Hazan's iconic Bolognese (the one where the ground chuck drinks up what must be a gallon of wine, milk, and tomato juice). In the summer, his happiest place is holding a gin and tonic while grilling a fleet of chicken thighs that have been steeping in an herby yogurt marinade all day. We both grew up in houses where dinner was defined as animal protein, starch, and vegetable, and even though we had half-heartedly been discussing cutting back on meat for years for our health and the planet's health, the truth was neither of us could really picture how it would look in our family of four—the two of us and our two teenagers. We had our family dinner routine, we liked our family dinner routine, and our family dinner routine worked. The readers of *Dinner: A Love Story*, the website and cookbook series that I'd been writing for a decade, seemed to be on the same page as us, consistently Instagramming

and sharing my recipes for Red Wine–Braised Short Ribs and Chicken Parm Meatballs and Roast Chicken, and visiting those pages way more frequently than, say, the baked Miso-Butter Tofu. Sure, there were more and more calls for vegetarian dinner ideas as the years went on, but if I am to believe my website's metrics, meat was still king.

In other words, I expected Andy to reply to my text with something like "Let me know how it goes" or "Good luck getting everyone on board with that one," but instead this is what he texted back:

*HIM:* Maybe, yeah.

*An opening.*

*HIM:* How would we do it?

*ME:* Maybe we try to cut back on meat during the week?

*HIM:* And eat meat only on weekends?

*ME:* Yeah, and if we go to someone's house or whatever and they're serving meat, we obviously eat it.

*HIM:* That sounds doable.

*HIM:* Are we pescatarians or vegetarians?

*ME:* We're not either yet.

*HIM:* Where does fish fit into this?

*ME:* Let's see how fast we run out of ideas.

*HIM:* What do we tell the girls?

*ME:* Do we have to tell the girls?

The girls are our daughters, Abby and Phoebe, who were fourteen and sixteen at the time of this exchange. They have their no-fly zones when it comes to certain foods—most notably, eggs (I know!!)—but for the most part, they are adventurous eaters and not the types to question a meal's legitimacy if it isn't anchored by a piece of animal protein. We had several meatless meals in our regular rotation already: black bean burritos with pickled onions, butternut squash soup, cold sesame noodles, pasta with caramelized onions and spinach, quesadillas, salad pizza, regular pizza. But those were the exceptions to the rule, single meals that broke up the meat-centric rotation of other favorites like chicken potpie, Uncle Tony's steak, barbecue chicken sandwiches, pork tacos. We wondered how they would do if the formula was reversed, if dinner as a rule was plant-based and the exception was chicken cutlets or pan-fried pork chops?

On the other hand, they are teenagers and, like most kids, are more game for things than we give them credit for. And though more often than not, the dinnertime conversation can dead-end with the usual flat-toned "fine" and "good" when they are asked about their days, there are nights when you realize they're teaching you far more than you are teaching them. Like, for instance, that you can use the word *fire* as an adjective. Or that Camus's philosophy can be distilled to one sentence: "Just because life is meaningless doesn't mean you can't give it meaning, and, Mom, there's too much mustard in this dressing." Or, this one, learned in earth science: "We could basically save the planet if we stopped eating beef."

I did know that actually, and I'm not proud of what I'm about to say, but there is something that feels way more urgent about a statistic like that when it comes out of the mouths of my own children, the ones who will be inheriting the planet that I have been complicit in neglecting and, let's be real, *destroying*. If there is something positive to spin from this, it's that their generation understands the broader significance of their food choices and is optimistic about making changes in a way that many of their parents are not. They are simultaneously motivated and motivating.

There were other factors that had been pushing us in the plant-based direction for a while now, too. Beyond the environmental implications, there were the personal ones: It has become almost impossible to watch our aging parents and not think about how we can take better care of our own middle-aged bodies. Using the same weekends-only strategy, we had already dialed back on drinking a few years ago and, just like other walking cliché midlife-crisis sufferers, started going to gym classes with names like "Gladiators" and "Core & More." Also helping things along was the fact that everywhere we look there seemed to be a big-name chef or cookbook author giving eggplant or Swiss chard or chickpeas the kind of star treatment once reserved for a pork shoulder or a leg of lamb. The "all-day café" trend happened in there somewhere, and lunches for work and with the family were suddenly happening over avocado toasts and smoothie bowls instead of burgers and turkey clubs.

But it's one thing to know you want to eat in a more plant-based direction and an entirely different thing to know how to execute that pledge night after night at the dinner table, especially if you are not a big-name chef, if you are just someone who is short on time and ideas but wants to do right by family dinnertime.

To complicate things further, I'd spent fifteen years nailing down the *exact* kinds of dinners my family would not only eat but greet with bona fide high-fives (and chronicling all of it very publicly!). I had found my rhythm and my repertoire—the salmon salad! The steak salad! Dad's cheeseburgers! Their Great-Great-Grandma Turano's meatballs, for crying out loud! That's two "greats" if you're not paying attention, which brings me to another point: Not only were these easy recipes that I could make on autopilot, they were sentimental family recipes that I figured would forever be associated with warm, happy memories of sitting around their childhood dinner table. One night, about a year and a half into our family's vegetarian pledge, over a plate of yogurt-y pasta and caramelized onions, my friend Joanna said to my daughters, "You're so lucky you're growing up in a house where the food is this good every night" (bless you, Joanna), before asking, "What would you say your parents' best dishes are?"

I mean, if there was ever a question tailored to make me feel like the greatest parent ever, this was it. Instead, Phoebe kind of shrugged and Abby looked like she was struggling to come up with an answer.

"I guess salmon salad," she said. "And salad pizza . . . since we're having a lot of that lately. And, um . . . that's kind of it."

I was incredulous. Part of me wanted to blame their responses on being teenagers—refusing to give their mother satisfaction in any way—but another side of me took a step back and thought about it. We had essentially overhauled our dinner table, and the expected answers to that question—pork ragu, turkey chili, sausage stromboli—the dinners that I pictured someday living on yellowed stained index cards in an antique recipe box labeled "Family Heirloom Recipes"—weren't exactly making a lot of appearances on the dinner table. And though I had developed many new vegetarian recipes that garnered thumbs-ups from both kids, were they heirloom-worthy the way that our pork ragù, with its own Instagram hashtag, was heirloom-worthy? Were they heirloom-worthy the way our milk-braised pork loin, *hand-painted on the inside of my kitchen cabinet* and one of the first dinners I shared with Andy when we met, was heirloom-worthy?

I'm not implying that a recipe has to have meat in it to be memorable—it's more that so many of the recipes in our repertoire for the first fifteen years of our children's lives happened to be meat-based. In other words, it was hard to just . . . move on from those. It felt like that day I decided to pack up the dollhouses cluttering their teenage bedrooms, sealing their childhoods into cardboard boxes while slowly having an emotional breakdown. I've never been terribly good at changes in eras, especially as they relate to my children, and this was no different. Which is why it took me so long to make the switch. *Next week*, I'd tell myself. *Next week would* for sure *be an entirely no-meat week*.

The day the lightning struck was the day I decided I needed to figure it out once and for all, and I thought the weekday vegetarian strategy would be a reasonable place to begin. Though nothing was written in blood, if I had to spell out the exact pledge it would've been something like this:

PART 1: We hereby promise to limit our meat consumption to weekends only, with *meat* defined as poultry, beef, and fish, and *weekend* defined as Saturday and Sunday—and the occasional Friday if we have reservations at that place famous for its burgers. If we are invited to someone's house for dinner, we will eat what we are served.

PART 2: For the grown-ups, the weekday vegetarian policy extends to breakfast and lunch; the kids, however, are free to make their own choices when out of the house. On nights when eggs (or anything else deemed equally offensive to kids) are served for dinner, the cook may use his or her discretion to supplement with a peanut butter sandwich, a drumstick slathered in barbecue sauce, a pan-fried sausage link, or any other food that can be easily prepared.

As you can see, we weren't exactly talking about an intense commitment, but I like to think this is why we were able to stick with it. In the beginning we were roasting a lot of those emergency drumsticks. I got in the habit of making extra turkey Bolognese on the weekend just so I could have it waiting in the wings in the freezer for those nights when someone at the table just couldn't face another refried bean quesadilla. I also developed a solid rotation

PIZZA WITH
CHEDDAR,
CARAMELIZED
ONION & EGG
(PAGE 34)

IT'S ONE THING TO KNOW YOU
WANT TO EAT IN A MORE PLANT-BASED
DIRECTION, IT'S AN ENTIRELY
DIFFERENT THING TO EXECUTE THAT
PLEDGE NIGHT AFTER NIGHT.

of flexitarian dinners that lent themselves to customizing. These meals—mostly multicomponent salads and "bowls"—reminded me of the toddler days when we sought out recipes that could be deconstructed into individual ingredients so everyone could pick and choose what they did and didn't want on their plates. In fact, that part of the process and those kinds of recipes were both crucial in the transition and the reason why you'll see notes on how to make recipes flexitarian throughout this book. (Look for the "For the Holdout" tag.) I'd be lying if I said that in the beginning we weren't regularly relying on those strategies. For the grown-ups as much as for the kids.

When my kids were little, I might've whined about this kind of cooking. Every new parent vows he or she is not going to be a short-order cook, catering to their children's whims and aversions like some kind of personal servant. I might've worried that by not forcing them to eat exactly what we were eating, they'd never learn how to eat properly and healthfully. These days, though, my strategic cooking makes me feel like everyone else in the world, whether a parent or not—that is, someone charged with simultaneously feeding carnivores, vegetarians, vegans, gluten-free eaters, Paleo eaters, keto faithfuls, flexitarians, and people who are thinking harder about the effects their choices have in the bigger picture (i.e., for Earth).

The goal of this book, as it has been for most of my food-writing career, is to continue simplifying dinnertime, to make this kind of cooking approachable, and to show that with a little planning and a lot of inspiration, it's possible to cut back on meat and not eat cornflakes every night. You'll find all the hallmarks typical of the meals in the *Dinner: A Love Story* orbit: strategic, healthy, creative, and—most important—realistic. When I'm coming up with recipe ideas, I ask myself if they pass the "text test," that is, is this recipe easy enough to text the basic idea to a friend? ("Sauté your garlic and onion, add red pepper flakes and white beans, puree it, top with pesto or croutons.") I know by now that we're not going to win anyone over to our weekday meat-free side with complicated recipes that require cooks to break out an army of small appliances on a Tuesday night. But even simple recipes take *some* work—it's still dinner and I'm not letting you off the hook completely here. The one hundred recipes in this book are solid, casual, healthy recipes that I *can* imagine texting to my friends without too many follow-up questions. They're the recipes that have convinced my family that plant-based eating is something we can stick with, and feel good about. I hope you'll pull up a chair and join us at the table.

*introduction: why now?*

BROILED CAESAR
SALAD WITH
CHICKPEAS (PAGE 69):
WE HAVE THIS
ONCE A WEEK.

# Am I allowed to Use this book on the weekend?

## & OTHER FAQS

**What's up with the title? Am I not allowed to use this book on the weekend?**

Of course you can use this book on the weekend, but you will most likely appreciate it more during the week. That's because the concept of *The Weekday Vegetarians* is twofold. First, it's a guiding strategy for people who are looking to scale back on meat but don't know where to begin. Setting realistic boundaries for yourself is helpful, and eating plant-based meals five nights a week is a significant, but not Draconian, way to help you along. (Think of it as Meatless Monday 2.0.) Second, as anyone with a job and/or a kid knows, weekday cooking—specifically week*night* cooking—is inherently different from weekend cooking. Even people who *love* to cook might not find themselves in the best frame of mind to cook for their families after a long day of work or in between sports and activities or with a toddler hanging on their hems. This collection provides "weekday" meals, because they are simple, easy-to-execute recipes that take this into account.

**OK, so where are the steak recipes for Saturday night?**

For those of you looking for meat-driven recipes to make on the weekend, you will not find them here, at least not in the traditional way. Throughout the recipe section, there will be suggestions for how to make various dishes more conducive for the vegetarian skeptic at your table—substitute chicken for the tofu here, add crumbled sausage with the beans there—so you won't end up falling back on meat as the anchor and catering to the lowest common "denomin-eater." I will say that the longer you stick with being a weekday vegetarian, the more you will notice plant-based eating creeping into your weekends and restaurant orders.

**What is the best way to use this book if I don't have a clue about what I want to make for dinner and everyone is ravenous?**

The recipes are organized by type of meal—pizza, pasta, soup, salad, and so on—but you can also search for a dinner idea based on the can of beans in the pantry or the bunch of kale in the crisper. Beginning on page 238, you'll find an ingredient-driven mix-and-match chart that will give you a sense of how I think about dinner. This should hopefully help you come up with something even on nights when you don't have what you need to make the exact recipes in this book.

**Are there any vegan recipes?**

Yes, there are a lot of them, and they're labeled very clearly. Also, throughout the book, you'll find instructions for how to transform vegetarian recipes into vegan ones.

**Why did you include Parmesan in this book?**

Authentic Parmesan, or Parmigiano Reggiano, which hails exclusively from the provinces of Parma, Reggio Emilia, and Modena, as well as parts of Bologna and Manua, is made using calf rennet and is therefore not considered vegetarian, something I'm embarrassed to say I learned only a few months before I started writing this book. You might not be surprised to hear that we have not completely banished it from our vegetarian nights, but we do think of it as a once-in-a-while ingredient. I'll use it to finish off a pizza or pasta, but otherwise I'll use nutritional yeast (an inactivated yeast that takes the form of yellow flakes and shares with Parmesan a remarkably similar salty depth) or vegetarian Grana or Parmesan. (Trader Joe's makes one, and you can generally find others in local supermarkets.) Throughout the book, you will see it listed simply as "Parmesan." I'll leave it to you to decide whether you want to opt for vegetarian Parmesan, nutritional yeast, or the real deal.

*am i allowed to use this book on the weekend?*

**Since *Dinner: A Love Story* (the website and book series) is usually all about family meals, does that mean this book is geared only toward people who are cooking for kids?**

Nope! Most recipes here are written to serve four, but, as always, I leave you to define who those four (or two or one) are at your table—just adjust measurements accordingly. Because I've been feeding kids (and writing about feeding kids) for so long, I can't help but suggest ideas and tricks for parents struggling to convince a skeptical preschooler to try, say, the lentils, but these dinners, like all my recipes, are not "kid recipes." First and foremost, they aim to be healthy, delicious, and easy to execute. Are there classic kid favorites like pizza and tacos and fritters here? Of course—because they happen to be my favorites, too. They are also wholesome, familiar crowd-pleasers that are genius gateways for convincing a meat-and-potatoes type of eater, no matter how old, to embrace something they might not have otherwise, like zucchini (Zucchini Pizza, page 38) or cauliflower (Spicy Cauliflower Fritters with Pea Shoots, page 129). Plus, saying that pizza is kids' food because it's made of dough and cheese is like saying Pixar movies are just for kids because they are animated. There are many, *many* ways to add layers of complexity to a dish and still make it appealing for everyone.

# Seven Rules to Remember When Going Vegetarian

## 1. Cook What You Know

You might want to start building a repertoire of vegetarian dinners by first thinking of ways to convert the recipes that you know and love into meatless versions. This could be as simple as omitting the sausage on your pizza or the chicken in your stir-fry. The goal, though, is to create a basic level of familiarity with the dish from both the cooking angle and the dining angle (and if you're cooking for kids, it will be less likely to incite a tableside revolt). This is especially important if you are serving people who like things A. Very. Specific. Way. For example, if you have been making and loving the same turkey chili for decades (as we have; see page 46), it might be worth starting with that recipe (swapping three bean varieties for the meat) instead of, say, debuting the silken tofu with fermented beans that you've been meaning to cook since 2003. Your made-over versions of favorite meals will most likely not taste exactly the same, but they will *look* mostly the same, and that's a head start. Going vegetarian doesn't mean anyone has to give up their favorite dish . . . just some of the ingredients involved in making that dish.

## 2. Build on Your Current Recipe Repertoire

Before this undertaking, as I've established, we ate a lot of meat. Like *a lot*—at least five times a week you'd find something chicken-, pork-, or beef-driven on our dinner plates. On the other hand, there were usually a few days a week when we ate vegetarian dinners without even thinking about it. Black bean burritos, barbecued baked beans, minestrone, salad pizzas, regular pizzas, macaroni and cheese, butternut squash soup, sesame noodles, pasta with basil pesto (all available on DinnerALoveStory.com) and on and on. They were major family favorites, and it was good to know that we could build our new way of eating around meals our kids already loved. Take a look at your own dinner rotation wearing vegetarian goggles and see what you come up with. I'll bet you're already further along than you think.

### 3. Don't Make It a Big Deal

Especially for those of you with young kids, who you wouldn't exactly describe as the adventurous type, don't make any loud proclamations about your new mostly vegetarian undertaking. In fact, maybe don't even mention it at all and see what happens. Sometimes, when you give something a name, it's easier to mount a campaign against it. Don't give them a cause. Give them noodles.

### 4. *Or . . .* Make It a *Huge* Deal

On the other hand, kids can be way more game to try new things than we give them credit for. When the girls were young, I decided to cook a brand-new dinner every night for thirty days straight (this was the premise of my second book, *Dinner: The Playbook*) and to spin the strategy as an adventure. We were going to try something brand-new every night! There would be charts and games and (don't tell all those baby food experts) even prizes if they tried new things! You know your family better than I do. If you think positioning weeknight vegetarian eating as something fun and important will help ease the change, pull out the PowerPoints and the pom-poms and officially launch your campaign.

### 5. Never Reveal the Meal Plan Ahead of Time

This is especially true if you're making something you know won't necessarily be received with open arms. The less time they have to organize their resistance, the better.

### 6. Use Your Hooks

There's an entire section (Part Three, pages 192–237) about this concept, but it's crucial to always have one thing on the plate that you or your potential convert is excited about, no matter how simple. If you're debuting Coconut Curried Red Lentils (page 162) for dinner, maybe consider frying up some homemade fresh Yogurt Flatbread (page 222) alongside them. (What, pray tell, is better than warm bread?) If you're steaming greens like spinach or kale for a side dish, think about drizzling some Spicy Peanut Sauce (page 203) on top. Your hooks could be crispy or mashed potatoes, a creamy ranch dressing, garlicky croutons on a salad, or buttery garlic bread on the side. They can even be store-bought hooks, like a can of Bush's baked beans or that bottled ginger-miso dressing your kid would drink like Gatorade if given the option. The point: Capitalize on the power of hooks to cast a warm, happy glow on the rest of the food on the plate.

## 7. Think Vegetable Forward, Not Just Vegetarian

Sure, most of us become interested in vegetarian eating because we want to cut back on meat, omit meat, or do our part to help minimize the environmental impact caused by the production of meat. But for me, another huge draw of going vegetarian was what I'd be *adding* to the dinner table, namely the vegetables themselves. If dialing down the meat means amping up the sugar snap peas in May, grilled Japanese eggplants in July, and caramelly Brussels sprouts in October, well, that's about as convincing an argument as I need. In other words, if you seek out the freshest in-season produce, you'll find the vegetables themselves are the best advocates for going vegetarian. I love building dinner around superstar in-season produce. *I have fresh asparagus, let's make that chilled asparagus soup. I have tomatoes and corn, let's make that show-stopper pasta* (page 87). And—decidedly less romantic but still just as relevant—*I have half a head of cabbage that's about to go bad, let's shred it and make Crispy Cabbage Pancakes* (page 132). It's a new way of thinking about dinner. Once you see how easy it is to use vegetables as a starting point (begin with Small Plates Night on page 146), you'll realize it's also extremely liberating.

PART
ONE

# the new regulars

**RECIPES FOR EVERYDAY DINNERS**

## WELCOME TO YOUR NEW FAVORITE DINNERS!

Besides being vegetarian, there is one thing that every recipe in this section has in common: They've all been served to my family—and served successfully. They were not dreamed up and developed in a test kitchen by a team of food editors. A real home cook made these dinners; real diners at a real table during real dinner hours ate them and, with few exceptions, genuinely enjoyed them.

Hopefully, they reflect the way we eat in a typical week, which is to say not exactly the same every single night. On Monday we might only be up for a bright blended soup made with tomatoes or asparagus or whatever is in season, then the next night crave pizza or a meaty mushroom pot pie. On Wednesday, everyone might be feeling cheesy, crowd-pleasing enchiladas, then the next night only be in the mood for a veg-packed vegan bowl. No matter what you're craving, you'll find something to match it in these pages. Unless that craving involves meat. Save that one for Saturday.

Before you start experimenting with the recipes, it's important for me to convey to you that the transition from mostly meat-based cooking to mostly plant-based cooking was not easy. It had been so thoroughly ingrained in my brain that a real meal was built around a piece of animal protein that, in the beginning, there were many weeknights when I'd surrender to the tabula rasa that was my dinner brain and just slather a few chicken thighs in mustard and panko the way my kids loved and make a salad while the chicken was roasting. *Tomorrow*, I'd tell myself. *Tomorrow, no meat.*

Things turned for me, though, when I realized that rather than focusing on meat as the central premise for dinner, I had to pay attention to the meal's "hook," a lightbulb-moment concept discovered on the night I now think of as the Tofu Massacre.

Here's what happened: I had just listened to a food podcast where the host had sung the praises of shredded tofu left and right and all around. Tofu had been a tough sell in our house, especially with my younger daughter, no matter how I prepared it for her—cubed, batoned, golden fried, stuffed into tacos, whirled in the food processor with vegetables and stuffed into wonton wrappers. No dice. This method sounded unique and promising—apparently, if you shred extra-firm tofu on the large-hole side of a cheese grater, it behaves very much like ground meat. Sounded good to me! I decided to try it out, folding my shreds into a stir-fry with my kids' favorite aromatics (garlic, ginger, onions) and flavors (soy sauce, rice vinegar), then loading the pan with vegetables. I didn't have a ton of vegetables, just some carrots and a little bit of broccoli, which I supplemented with a handful of frozen peas.

It was a disaster. (Probably because I had only half-heartedly followed the podcaster's instructions.) The vegetables were diced too small, so they cooked quickly, and when I folded them in with the tofu, the whole thing kind of meshed together in a way that made it look and taste like an adult meal that had been blended for a toothless toddler. It was not my best effort, and I knew this even before I looked at my kids, both of whom had faces so contorted they looked like they'd just been forced to chug black-market moonshine.

"What's for dinner tomorrow?" one of them asked mid-gag, probably hoping to capitalize on the epic fail in order to convince me to plan on cheeseburgers.

Their postmortem comments were constructive, though. While we were cleaning up the crime scene, Abby said to me, "You know why this one didn't work?"

Did I want to know?

"It didn't work because there was nothing in this meal that I was excited about eating." That was putting it nicely. "What I mean," she continued, "is that usually there's something crispy or saucy, or something like a buttery potato or cheese on toast or crispy broccoli or teriyaki onions or some creamy sauce or something you know I'll eat no matter what. This was all just kind of mushed together and—"

"I get it." I cut her off before she could continue. "The meal needs some sort of hook."

"Yes," she said. "A hook!"

Abby wasn't saying she needed her dinner to come with french fries and a Coke; she was saying something that we all know subconsciously: that is, if there is even just one component—and not even a particularly large serving of that component—of the meal that is exciting or slightly indulgent, it has the potential to cast a glow over the rest of the plate. It could be a small side of Andy's Spicy Diced Potatoes (page 182) alongside the bean burritos, or it could even just be the Caesar Dressing (page 204) Abby and Phoebe love drizzled over a shredded kale salad. As it was, with a meal like the Tofu Massacre, my daughters' taste buds were searching in vain for something to attach themselves to, coming up short, then flaming out in failure.

I started to think about the components of meals that we are *all* excited about eating, and the more success I had with meals made around those components, the more I started thinking about those as my new building blocks. Where I used to develop a meal based on the chicken or ground turkey that was in my fridge, I started training myself to think about my family's *hooks*, the ingredients and components that everyone looked forward to eating, even if they took up only one small corner of the plate. Some of these hooks were proteins (crispy chickpeas, refried beans); some of them were not necessarily nutrient-rich (hand-torn croutons, creamy polenta, homemade flatbread); some of them were sauces and glazes that could be made ahead of time (miso-tahini, sweet chili, spicy peanut); some of them were as simple as a spice mixture picked up at the local Japanese market (hello, *furikake*). Each of them at one point or another got me through a rough patch, and they have their own special section in this book (pages 199 to 233) because they have some sort of magical hold on my family.

You'll see me refer to them again and again in the dinner recipe pages, and I encourage you to think about your own family's hooks, which might be different from ours.

RIGHT

A NO-RECIPE RECIPE: FARRO (PAGE 234) WITH ROASTED BEETS, FETA, DILL, AND ALL-PURPOSE VINAIGRETTE (PAGE 217).

# pizzas

# PIZZA with CHEDDAR, CARAMELIZED ONION & EGG

You want the onions here to be sweet and jammy, which takes roughly 20 to 25 minutes, but if you don't have that kind of time on a weeknight, you can always do what my friend and gifted food writer Frances Boswell taught me: Pull them off the stovetop when you have to, and stir in a few drops of balsamic vinegar to get a similar depth. Note: This recipe calls for 4 eggs, one in each corner, but if you want to serve 6 pieces of pizza, each with an egg, add more eggs and space them out accordingly. I like to pair this with a simple green salad.

5 tablespoons extra-virgin olive oil

3 large yellow onions, roughly chopped

1 (16-ounce) pizza dough (store-bought is fine), at room temperature for at least 30 minutes and up to 3 hours (this makes it easier to work with)

¼ teaspoon garlic powder

6 ounces sharp cheddar, grated (about 1½ cups) or sliced

4 large eggs (or more to taste; see Note above)

Kosher salt and freshly ground black pepper to taste

Chopped fresh flat-leaf parsley, for garnish

Preheat the oven to 450°F. Arrange an oven rack in the middle position.

As the oven heats, combine 3 tablespoons of the olive oil and the onions in a large skillet set over medium-low heat. (The skillet should be big enough to hold the onions mostly in one layer; they will cook faster this way.) Stir every few minutes, making sure they are getting soft and golden but not blackened or burned, until caramel colored and slightly jammy, 20 to 25 minutes.

While the onions are cooking, brush an 18 × 13-inch sheet pan with 1 tablespoon of the olive oil. Drop the dough in the center of the pan and, using your fingers, press and stretch out the dough to the sides and into corners of the pan. The goal is to get the crust as thin as possible. Mix together the garlic powder and the remaining tablespoon olive oil and brush the perimeter of the dough.

Top the dough with an even layer of the cheddar, leaving a 1-inch cheese-free border, and bake for 8 minutes. Remove from the oven and top with the caramelized onions, shaping them into 4 (or more; see Note) little "nests" for the eggs in each corner. Carefully crack 1 egg in each nest. Bake until the whites are cooked, the yolks are still slightly runny, and the pizza crust is golden, about 5 minutes. Top with salt, pepper, and parsley.

# ARTICHOKE DIP PIZZA

This is the happy result of someone in my house asking, "What would happen if we turned that classic artichoke dip into a pizza?" Answer: How could it be bad? If you want to kick up the green quotient, add an extra ½ cup thawed frozen chopped spinach to the artichoke mixture.

2 tablespoons extra-virgin olive oil

1 (16-ounce) pizza dough (store-bought is fine), at room temperature for at least 30 minutes and up to 3 hours (this makes it easier to work with)

¼ teaspoon garlic powder

1 (14-ounce) can artichoke hearts, drained and chopped roughly

½ cup thawed frozen spinach, squeezed completely dry

¼ cup mayonnaise

1 cup part-skim shredded mozzarella

½ cup grated Parmesan cheese (about 1½ ounces)

1 teaspoon Worcestershire sauce

Chopped fresh flat-leaf parsley, for garnish (optional)

Preheat the oven to 475°F. Arrange an oven rack in the middle position.

Brush an 18 × 13-inch sheet pan with 1 tablespoon of the olive oil. Drop the dough in the center of the sheet pan and, using your fingers, press and stretch out the dough to the sides and into the corners of the pan. (If you prefer a thicker, chewier crust, form the dough into a round shape, as shown.) Mix together the garlic powder and the remaining tablespoon olive oil and brush the perimeter of the dough.

In a medium bowl, mix together the artichoke hearts, spinach, mayonnaise, mozzarella, Parmesan, and Worcestershire. Spread the mixture over the crust in a thin layer, leaving a 1-inch border.

Bake on the oven's middle rack until the cheese is bubbly and the crust is golden, about 15 minutes. (Keep an eye on it.) Let rest 5 minutes so it's easier to cut. Top with parsley, if using.

pizza

# ZUCCHINI PIZZA

I have a house of zucchini haters—actually that's not fair; I'll call them zucchini *tolerators*. This recipe, though, *this* recipe was delicious enough to make them rethink their position, which probably had something to do with the fact that my inspiration came directly from Rome's legendary Forno Campo de' Fiori pizzeria. The key is to expel as much liquid from the shredded zucchini as possible before baking, and also not to be stingy with the fresh herbs. I also love that this pizza is 100 percent uncompromised—better even—if you serve it at room temperature, casually on parchment paper in the middle of a picnic table. If you are doing that, hold off on finishing with the mint (which will blacken when warmed) until the pizza has fully cooled or right before you serve.

SERVES 4

38

pizzas

**4 to 5 cups shredded zucchini (from 2 medium zucchini, any color), pressed with paper towels or wrung dry in a kitchen towel**

**⅓ cup extra-virgin olive oil, plus more for coating and drizzling**

**2 small cloves garlic, pressed or finely minced**

**Leaves from 3 fresh thyme sprigs**

**Pinch of dried red pepper flakes**

**Kosher salt and freshly ground black pepper to taste**

**1 (16-ounce) pizza dough (store-bought is fine), at room temperature for at least 30 minutes and up to 3 hours (this makes it easier to work with)**

**6 ounces fresh mozzarella, torn into small pieces**

**⅓ cup freshly grated Parmesan cheese**

### SERVING

**2 tablespoons torn fresh mint leaves (from 8 to 10 leaves)**

**3 ounces fresh ricotta (about ⅓ cup)**

**Sea salt**

Preheat the oven to 475°F.

In a large mixing bowl, toss together the zucchini, olive oil, garlic, thyme, red pepper flakes, salt, and black pepper. Brush an 18 × 13-inch rimmed sheet pan with a thin coat of olive oil. Drop the dough in the center of the sheet pan and, using your fingers, press and stretch out the dough to flatten it so it reaches as close as possible to all four corners. The goal is to get the crust as thin as possible.

Evenly arrange the mozzarella pieces on the dough (you don't have to cover all the dough with cheese), leaving a 1-inch border. Using your hands, distribute zucchini over the dough (except the border), then, using a pastry brush, brush the perimeter of the crust with whatever olive oil remains at the bottom of the zucchini bowl (add up to a tablespoon more, if necessary). Sprinkle the Parmesan evenly on top of the zucchini. Bake for 15 to 18 minutes, until the crust looks golden and the cheese is bubbly. Let cool slightly so it's easier to slice. When ready to serve, top with the mint, dollops of ricotta, and more freshly ground black pepper and sea salt.

# COBB SALAD PIZZA

We make two "salad pizzas" on repeat in my house: one where we top a warm, just-baked tomato-saucy pizza dough with chopped romaine lettuce, tomatoes, red onion, a little shredded Parm, and oregano-spiked Pizza Dressing (page 215), which has a long and loyal following on my website. The other? This one below, pizza-fied Cobb salad, which, truth be told, originally appeared on our table with prosciutto or cooked bacon draped in between the lettuce shreds. In that way, like most pizzas, it's a good recipe to have in your flexitarian repertoire—you can serve a vegetarian holdout a slice with bacon to keep the peace without compromising your own weeknight vegetarian principles.

3 tablespoons unsalted butter

3 tablespoons all-purpose flour

¾ cup milk

Kosher salt and freshly ground black pepper to taste

1 garlic clove, minced or pressed

1 cup crumbled blue cheese (about 4 ounces)

¼ teaspoon red pepper flakes (or more to taste)

½ cup extra-virgin olive oil, plus more for greasing

1 (16-ounce) pizza dough (store-bought is fine), at room temperature for at least 30 minutes and up to 3 hours (this makes it easier to work with)

Corn kernels from 2 medium ears (about 1 cup), uncooked

2 tablespoons finely minced red onion

¼ cup red wine vinegar

1 tablespoon fresh lemon juice (from ½ small lemon)

Squeeze of honey

1 romaine heart, shredded with a knife

1 cup chopped tomatoes (any kind)

2 tablespoons chopped chives

Preheat the oven to 475°F.

Make the sauce: Melt the butter in a saucepan over medium-low heat. Whisk in the flour until the mixture is smooth, and let cook another minute, whisking the whole time. Whisk in the milk, salt, and pepper, and cook until slightly thickened. Remove from the heat and stir in the garlic, blue cheese, and red pepper flakes. Let cool slightly.

Using your fingers or a pastry brush, grease an 18 × 13-inch sheet pan with some olive oil. Drop the dough in the center of the sheet pan and, using your fingers, press and stretch it out to the sides and as close as possible into the corners. The goal is to get the dough as thin as possible. Using a rubber spatula, smooth the blue cheese sauce across the top of the dough, leaving a 1-inch perimeter. Scatter the corn and red onion on top. Brush the perimeter of the dough with more olive oil and bake until the crust is crispy and golden, 12 to 15 minutes.

While the crust is baking, make your salad. In a large bowl, whisk together the oil, vinegar, lemon juice, honey, salt, and pepper. Toss in the lettuce, tomatoes, and chives.

When the pizza crust has finished baking, let it cool slightly, about 5 minutes, then top with the salad. (To prevent a soggy crust and oily fingers, use tongs to distribute the salad, making sure excess dressing does not spill onto the pizza.) Cut the pizza and serve with a lot of napkins.

THE PUPS KNOW
A GOOD THING WHEN
THEY SEE IT.

# bowls & salads

# BLACK RICE BOWLS with OMELET RIBBONS & SNOW PEAS

Sure, you could just as easily make this with regular sushi rice, but substituting black rice seasoned with furikake—the sesame-seeded, seaweed-salty Japanese spice blend—is what makes this weeknight meal extra special (and extra nutty), without hardly any more effort expended. As for the omelet ribbons: Again, the most humble of ingredients (an egg) takes on a whole new identity when cooked into several thin omelets that are then stacked, rolled, and sliced into feathery fettuccine-like strands, a process I first read about from food and travel writer Heidi Swanson. It takes a little practice to get the hang of flipping the superthin eggs, but don't be discouraged. Even if you mess up and have to serve the bowl with bits of broken omelet, it will still taste delicious.

1 cup black rice, rinsed

4 tablespoons seasoned rice vinegar

4 tablespoons soy sauce

7 large eggs

2 tablespoons mirin

Pinch of kosher salt

1 teaspoon toasted sesame oil

1 teaspoon canola oil (spray works, too), plus more as necessary

### SERVING

1 bunch scallions, light green and white parts only, minced (about ⅔ cup)

2 cups trimmed and horizontally sliced sugar snap peas

Vegetarian furikake (look for one that does not contain dried fish)

Toasted sesame seeds

Cook the rice according to the package directions. Drizzle 3 tablespoons of the vinegar into the hot rice slowly, tossing the rice with a fork. Combine the remaining rice wine vinegar and 3 tablespoons of the soy sauce in a small bowl for the drizzling sauce. Set aside.

While the rice cooks, heat a medium nonstick skillet over medium-low heat. In a bowl, whisk the eggs with the remaining soy sauce, mirin, and salt. Add the oils to the skillet, using a brush to coat the entire surface. Pour in one-quarter of the egg mixture, rotating the pan so the egg spreads out as paper-thinly as possible. Once the egg is cooked through, which shouldn't take more than 20 seconds, slip a rubber spatula under one side and a metal spatula under the other side, then carefully flip the omelet and cook another 15 to 20 seconds. The goal is to create a very delicate omelet with zero-to-minimal browning. Slide the omelet onto a cutting board. Repeat with the remainder of the batter, adding more oil as necessary, stacking omelets on the cutting board as you go. Once you've cooked all the egg mixture, roll the stacked omelets into a log and slice them crosswise into very thin ribbonlike strands.

Divide the rice among four bowls and top with the egg ribbons, scallions, sugar snap peas, furikake, toasted sesame seeds, and drizzling sauce.

# THREE-BEAN CHILI BOWLS
## with CHOCOLATE & PLANTAIN CHIPS

Sometimes we get lucky and just swap a vegetable for meat in a favorite recipe and no one is any worse for the wear, like the Cauliflower Cutlets with Romesco Sauce on page 144. Other times, like with a turkey chili we've been making since the girls were in diapers, we have to slowly get them used to the idea that a beloved meal is not going to taste exactly the same. In the case of our turkey chili, which already called for black beans, we just kept gradually changing the ratio of turkey to beans in favor of the beans. (The inclusion of dark chocolate, inspired by traditional moles, helps replicate a little of the depth that was missing once the meat completely disappeared.) We also switched out crumbled tortilla chips for plantain chips—a favorite snack we always have lying around. They add a nice sweetness along with the necessary crunch. Eventually everyone came around.

3 tablespoons oil (any kind: olive, canola, whatever)

1 medium yellow onion, chopped

1 garlic clove, minced

Kosher salt and freshly ground black pepper to taste

Dash of dried red pepper flakes, or to taste

1 tablespoon tomato paste

1½ cups cooked kidney beans, or 1 (15-ounce) can, rinsed and drained

1½ cups cooked pinto beans, or 1 (15-ounce) can, rinsed and drained

1½ cups cooked black beans, or 1 (15-ounce) can, rinsed and drained (you can drain and rinse all beans in the same colander)

¼ cup chili powder, or 2 teaspoons adobo sauce from canned chipotle chiles in adobo sauce (this is the spicier option!)

1 (28-ounce) can diced tomatoes, with juice

1 ounce dark chocolate, roughly chopped

2 teaspoons dried oregano

1 dried bay leaf

Dash of ground cinnamon

### SERVING

Plantain chips

Pickled Onions (page 231)

Avocado chunks

Sour cream (omit for vegans)

Shredded cheddar (omit for vegans)

Hot sauce

Chopped fresh cilantro

Heat the oil in a medium pot set over medium-low heat. Add the onion, garlic, salt, black pepper, and red pepper flakes and cook, stirring every now and then, until the onion is translucent, about 4 minutes. Stir in the tomato paste and cook another minute, until the tomato paste darkens slightly. Add the beans and chili powder, turn the heat to medium-high, and cook until the spices get sizzly, about 3 more minutes.

Add the tomatoes, chocolate, oregano, bay leaf, and cinnamon and bring to a boil. Turn the heat to low and simmer, stirring occasionally, until the flavors have a chance to deepen and meld together, about 30 minutes. Serve in bowls with plantain chips and your desired toppings.

FOR THE
*holdout*

STIR IN COOKED CHICKEN
CHORIZO SAUSAGE
CRUMBLES OR COOKED
GROUND BEEF.

/ vegan /

# BARLEY BOWLS *with* CHICKPEAS, ROASTED VEGETABLES & AVOCADO DRESSING

I can't say this happens in every family, but as my daughters approached the end of high school and I saw less and less of them, I started using dinner as leverage ("Too bad you're not home tonight because we're having those spicy potatoes you like so much"), if not as downright bribes ("Please be home! I'll make you anything you want"). I also offered tailor-made requests, no matter how fussy or involved, so they'd be more personally invested—and that's how I found myself asking them one night, "If you could have a grain bowl with anything on it, what would it be, sky's the limit?" The answer to that is the recipe you see below. There's a lot going on flavorwise—it's roasty, creamy, pickly, and 100 percent vegan to boot. As with most bowl dinners, it is a little more involved than you think, and it always helps to have a few of the components made ahead of time if you want to get it on the table fast. On the other hand, I'll hull the barley myself if it means my daughters are guaranteed to sit down with me and eat.

### THE BOWLS

1 cup uncooked pearled barley

12 ounces Brussels sprouts, halved (about 4 cups)

12 ounces chopped broccoli florets (about 4 cups)

¼ cup extra-virgin olive oil

Kosher salt and freshly ground black pepper to taste

3 cups Crispy Chickpeas (page 198) or store-bought, such as Saffron Road brand

Pickled Onions (page 231)

### THE DRESSING

1 ripe avocado, peeled and pitted

¼ cup extra-virgin olive oil

3 tablespoons white wine vinegar or distilled white vinegar

½ teaspoon honey or agave for vegans

2 tablespoons fresh lemon juice (from ½ medium lemon)

Kosher salt and freshly ground black pepper to taste

Preheat the oven to 425°F.

**PREPARE THE BOWLS:** In a medium pot, combine the barley and 3 cups water. Bring to a boil, then decrease the heat to low and keep it at the laziest simmer. Cover and cook, checking for doneness after 30 minutes. You want the grains to be tripled in size and tender but not mushy. If there is still water left in the pot when they've reached this point—keeping in mind you might have to let them cook another 5 to 10 minutes—you can strain the barley in a colander, the way you strain pasta.

Meanwhile, in a large bowl, toss together the Brussels sprouts, broccoli, olive oil, and some salt and pepper. Spread them out in an even layer on a sheet pan and roast for 20 to 25 minutes, until everything is crispy and browned.

**MAKE THE DRESSING:** Meanwhile, in a small food processor, whirl together the avocado, olive oil, vinegar, honey, lemon juice, 2 tablespoons water, and some salt and pepper. The final consistency should be thin enough to drizzle, so add more water as necessary. Adjust seasoning to taste.

Divide the barley evenly among four bowls and top with the roasted vegetables, crispy chickpeas, and pickled onions. Drizzle with avocado dressing and serve.

/ vegan /

# A FARROTTO for ALL SEASONS

I knew farrotto—the dish where nutrient-rich farro is prepared like risotto—was going to be a rotation staple as soon as the early reviews came in. "Tastes like *cacio e pepe*," said Abby. To that I'd add, "But healthier." We use this recipe as a template all year long, throwing in whatever vegetables are at their best. (The suggested summer version with corn, golden tomatoes, and basil is a particular favorite.) Like regular risotto, the dish takes a little stovetop babysitting, but it's the kind of mindless work you can do while reading a book or sipping a glass of wine. Add a Seven-Minute Egg (page 197) if you want a protein hit.

2 tablespoons extra-virgin olive oil

2 tablespoons unsalted butter

½ small onion, chopped

Kosher salt and freshly ground black pepper to taste

Dash of dried red pepper flakes

2 cups pearled farro

½ cup dry white wine

4 cups vegetable stock, store-bought or homemade (page 232), warmed

Seasonal vegetables and an herb (see Add-ins below)

⅔ cup grated Parmesan cheese

Combine the olive oil and 1 tablespoon of the butter in a deep medium-size skillet over medium heat. Add the onion, salt, black pepper, and red pepper flakes and cook until the onion is softened, stirring occasionally, about 3 minutes. Stir in the farro and wine and increase the heat to medium-high. Stir until most of the wine has been absorbed, then start adding vegetable stock in 1-cup drizzles, adding more as the liquid is absorbed. (You want the grains to always be just slightly submerged.) This is when you should prepare your seasonal vegetable add-in (see below). When the farro is cooked (porridgy but still a little toothy, like risotto, 30 to 35 minutes), turn off the heat and stir in the remaining tablespoon butter, the Parmesan, and the desired vegetable combination. Serve the farrotto in bowls topped with the suggested fresh herb.

## SEASONAL ADD-INS

*SUMMER:* 1 cup quartered cherry tomatoes and the uncooked kernels from 2 medium ears of corn; finish with chopped fresh basil

*FALL:* Roasted Honeynut Squash with Crispy Sage Leaves (page 188)

*WINTER:* 3 cups halved Brussels sprouts, tossed with 3 tablespoons extra-virgin olive oil, salt, and black pepper, and roasted at 425°F for 12 minutes; ½ cup frozen peas; finish with fresh thyme or tarragon

*SPRING:* 8 ounces sliced mushrooms, such as cremini, shiitake, or white button, sautéed in 2 tablespoons extra-virgin olive oil with salt and pepper until crispy (about 10 minutes); about a dozen and a half trimmed, chopped asparagus (you can add them to the mushrooms toward the last few minutes of cooking); and a teaspoon of lemon zest; finish with chopped fresh flat-leaf parsley

 FOR THE holdout / ADD COOKED CRUMBLED SAUSAGE OR SHRIMP FOR ANY RESISTERS.

# SPICY-TANGY-SMOKY PINTO BEAN BOWLS

Last year, my kids returned from a visit to Chipotle with a request: "Can you make the pinto beans as good as they do? *They're so tangy and smoky.*" I love when they issue challenges to me, because it usually means they become way more invested in their own tableside victories. To replicate the smokiness, I initially tried a version with dried ancho chili peppers, which was delicious but involved rehydrating the peppers with boiling water and breaking out the blender to puree them until smooth. I wanted a shortcut version—one that didn't take the same amount of time as driving to Chipotle—and ended up relying on smoked paprika instead. I was delighted by the result. Speaking of cutting corners: Many of the components in the finished bowls can be either homemade or store-bought—you just have to figure out what you have the time and energy for. If you don't have time to mash avocado, chopped onions, and cilantro into guacamole, slices of avocado will suffice; if you don't have time to make rice, the freezer pouches you can heat on the stovetop in five minutes (or in the microwave) will be fine. I do recommend including at least one topping that is fresh and bright—either the homemade Salsa Fresca (page 209) or the crunchy, raw shredded lettuce.

3 tablespoons neutral oil (such as canola or vegetable, or extra-virgin olive oil in a pinch)

½ small yellow onion, chopped

Kosher salt and freshly ground black pepper to taste

1 large garlic clove, minced

1 tablespoon plus 1 teaspoon smoked paprika

2 teaspoons tomato paste

Pinch of cayenne pepper (optional)

3 cups cooked pinto beans, or 2 (15-ounce) cans, rinsed and drained

3 tablespoons red wine vinegar

*SERVING OPTIONS*

4 cups cooked rice (any kind)

Guacamole

Sour cream (omit for vegans)

Cilantro

Shredded lettuce tossed with grapeseed or extra virgin olive oil and red wine vinegar

Shredded sharp cheddar cheese (omit for vegans)

Sliced radishes

Salsa Fresca (page 209)

Minced red onions

In a medium pot set over medium heat, combine
the oil, onion, salt, and black pepper and cook
until the onion is soft, about 3 minutes. Add
the garlic, paprika, tomato paste, and cayenne
(if using), stirring everything together and
allowing the tomato paste to sizzle and toast.
Toss in the beans and ½ cup water (or bean
cooking liquid if you home-cooked your beans)
and heat until everything has warmed through,
5 to 6 minutes. Remove from the heat and stir
in the vinegar. (The beans should be slightly
stewy; if they aren't, add a little more water to
loosen them up.) Serve with cooked rice and
your desired toppings.

/ vegan /

# EGGPLANT & TOFU
## with SWEET-HOT CHILI GLAZE

I am addicted to this sweet-and-spicy bowl, but if you find it's too fiery for your charges, it also works with Teriyaki Sauce (page 211). (Using the teriyaki makes this recipe vegan, I just omit the honey.) Whichever one you choose, make it while the tofu and eggplants roast. If you are lucky enough to find smaller Fairy Tale eggplants, halve each lengthwise and roast, cut-side down, so they get all brown and glossy. Note: This is a light meal—serve with basmati or brown rice if you want to stretch it out.

1 (14- to 15-ounce) block extra-firm tofu, pressed, drained, and cubed (see page 237)

½ cup olive oil

2 tablespoons soy sauce

1 tablespoon cornstarch

1 pound eggplants, preferably Graffiti, cubed

Kosher salt and freshly ground black pepper to taste

⅓ cup Sweet-Hot Chili Glaze (page 210)

4 cups cooked rice (any kind; optional)

### SERVING

Chopped scallions, white and light green parts only

Sliced radishes

Chopped fresh cilantro

Roasted cashews, chopped

Preheat the oven to 425°F. Arrange one oven rack in the upper position and another in the middle position. Line two sheet pans with parchment paper.

In a large bowl, toss the tofu cubes with ¼ cup of the olive oil, the soy sauce, and cornstarch. Using a slotted spoon, place the tofu on one of the prepared sheet pans.

In the same bowl, toss the eggplant with the remaining olive oil, the salt and pepper, and whatever remains from the tofu tossing. Place the eggplant on the other prepared sheet pan.

Place the sheet pan with the tofu on the top rack of the oven and the eggplant one on the middle rack. Bake until the tofu looks crispy and golden, 15 to 20 minutes. Remove the tofu from the oven and transfer it to a shallow serving bowl. Move the sheet pan with the eggplant to the top rack and continue to roast until the cubes look roasted and golden, another 10 to 15 minutes.

Remove the eggplant from the oven and transfer it to the bowl with the tofu. Drizzle 3 tablespoons of the glaze over the tofu-eggplant mixture, gently tossing so every piece is covered.

Serve plain or with rice and have each diner garnish with desired toppings.

# GLAZED MAITAKE MUSHROOMS
## *with* SWEET CORN POLENTA

Maitake mushrooms (also known as hen-of-the-woods) can be pricey, but when they're roasted, they look like short ribs and taste just as meaty and flavorful. (Well, almost.) I find it's best to make this meal in the early fall when corn and tomatoes are still sweet and the slight evening chill has you craving hearty comfort food. You can just as easily use your favorite kind of mushroom here if maitakes are unavailable or too much of an investment, and no one would arrest you for adding a Seven-Minute Egg (page 197) on top. I like to make the creamy polenta while the vegetables are roasting.

2 cups tomatoes (any kind, any size), halved

2 tablespoons extra-virgin olive oil

Kosher salt and freshly ground black pepper to taste

1 medium leek, cleaned and chopped

12 to 15 ounces maitake mushrooms, broken into largish chunks (about 8 total; you want 2 per person)

4 tablespoons Sweet-Hot Chili Glaze (page 210)

Sweet, Creamy Polenta (page 228)

### SERVING

Chopped fresh herbs, such as chives, thyme leaves, and/or tarragon

Preheat the oven to 425°F. Line a sheet pan with foil.

In a large bowl, toss the tomatoes with 1 tablespoon of the olive oil and some salt and pepper. Place the tomatoes on the prepared sheet pan and roast for 15 minutes.

Meanwhile, in the same large bowl, toss the leeks and mushrooms with the remaining 1 tablespoon olive oil, 2 tablespoons of the chili glaze, and some salt and pepper. Once the tomatoes have roasted for 15 minutes, push them to the perimeter of the sheet pan and add the leeks and mushrooms in the center. Roast everything 10 minutes more, flipping the leeks and mushrooms halfway through so both sides look brown and caramelly and the tomatoes are bursting and shriveled.

Divide the polenta among four bowls and top with the mushrooms, leeks, and tomatoes. Drizzle with the remaining 2 tablespoons chili glaze and top with the fresh herbs.

# CIDER-BRAISED CABBAGE WEDGES *with* POLENTA

I have always loved cabbage, but that love kicked into a higher gear during the quarantine of 2020. No matter what variety I stocked up on (savoy, napa, green, red), it lasted forever, and often I found myself building entire meals around it when we had run out of almost everything else. In my meat-eating days, I had mostly appreciated cabbage when shredded in a slaw and served next to, say, barbecued chicken. But once I discovered that a wedge could take on a new caramelized life in the oven, resulting in meals that were just as satisfying as, say, that barbecued chicken, the humble side-dish vegetable got promoted to Main Dish. This sweet-and-sour take is particularly homey and warm-your-bones good in the winter or early spring.

⅓ cup extra-virgin olive oil

1 medium head green or savoy cabbage (about 2 pounds), divided into 4 wedges, core intact

Kosher salt and freshly ground black pepper to taste

2 tablespoons unsalted butter or olive oil (for vegans)

2 garlic cloves, minced

1 large red onion, sliced

1 tablespoon tomato paste

½ cup apple cider vinegar

½ cup apple cider

1 cup vegetable stock, store-bought or homemade (page 232)

1 tablespoon honey

Sweet, Creamy Polenta (page 228)

SERVING

Chopped fresh chives or flat-leaf parsley

*To veganize*

SERVE WITH RICE INSTEAD OF POLENTA AND REPLACE THE HONEY WITH MAPLE SYRUP.

Preheat the oven to 350°F.

Heat the olive oil in a large ovenproof skillet set over medium-high heat. Cook the cabbage wedges in the oil, until each side is golden brown, 6 to 8 minutes per side. Remove to a platter and season with salt and pepper.

To the same pan, add the butter, garlic, onion, salt, and pepper. Reduce the heat to medium, and cook, stirring occasionally, until the onion and garlic are softened, about 5 minutes.

Stir in the tomato paste and cook until the color deepens and the whole thing smells toasty, about 2 minutes. Stir in the cider vinegar, cider, vegetable stock, and honey. Simmer about 10 minutes to reduce the liquid slightly, then nestle the cabbage wedges back into the skillet, adding enough water so the liquid reaches halfway up the wedges (about ¾ cup).

Transfer the skillet to the oven and bake, uncovered, until the cabbage is tender and caramelized around the edges, about 45 minutes, using tongs to gently turn the wedges halfway through cooking (it's inevitable that they will fall apart a little, but that's fine).

Divide the polenta among four bowls. Top each serving with a cabbage wedge and some of the sauce from the pan and finish with chopped herbs.

# CHOOSE-YOUR-OWN-ADVENTURE SPICY TOFU CRUMBLES

Back when my dinner default mode was chicken or chicken, I used to walk into the house at 6:30 p.m., cube some breasts and pan-fry them in a cast-iron skillet with onion, garlic, chili powder, and oregano. While they were cooking, I'd play choose-your-own-adventure—should we have them stuffed into hard-shell tacos? Served over rice? Turned into enchiladas? Tossed into a salad with avocado, tomatoes, and black beans? This method gave me a solid building block, and when we went vegetarian, I craved something like it to take its place. These spicy tofu crumbles are the answer. Use them as a starting point for all of the same meals mentioned above.

1 (14- to 15-ounce) block extra-firm tofu, drained

¼ cup extra-virgin olive oil

Kosher salt and freshly ground black pepper to taste

2 garlic cloves, minced

3 tablespoons chopped yellow onion

2 tablespoons chili powder

1 teaspoon dried oregano

1 tablespoon tomato paste

/ vegan /

Using your hands, squeeze the tofu like a sponge to expel as much liquid as possible and breaking it into crumbles as you do this. Place the pieces on a paper-towel-lined plate as it breaks, then pat them dry with another paper towel. (The more liquid you expel, the easier it will be to crisp up the tofu.)

Heat the olive oil in a large nonstick skillet over medium-high heat. Add the tofu then season with salt and pepper and cook undisturbed until browned, about 3 minutes. Toss, scraping up anything sticking to the pan, and continue to cook until the crumbles are golden brown and crisp around the edges, another 3 to 4 minutes. Push the tofu to the side of the pan and add the garlic and onion, cooking until the onion starts to soften, another few minutes.

Decrease the heat to medium. Stir everything together, then add the chili powder and oregano and cook until the spices get deep in color, about 3 minutes. Stir in the tomato paste, then add ¼ cup water. Cook until the tomato paste is distributed and warmed through, about 2 minutes.

## Now! Choose Your Own Adventure

**SIMPLE BOWLS:** *Serve the crumbles over white rice and top with queso fresco (omit if vegan), cilantro, and chopped scallions (white and light green parts only).*

**TACOS:** *Stuff crumbles inside soft tortillas or hard shells (my kids' fave) with avocado, shredded cabbage, and sour cream (omit if vegan).*

**SALADS:** *Let the tofu cool a bit, then toss it with black beans, avocado, fresh tomatoes, and citrus vinaigrette (replace the vinegar in All-Purpose Vinaigrette, page 217, with 1 tablespoon each fresh lime and orange juice and increase the lemon juice to 2 tablespoons).*

# QUINOA with ROASTED WINTER VEGETABLES

For a while, quinoa had fallen out of the rotation in our house because we became so enamored by the trendier, shinier wheat berry and farro grains. But ever since the height of its U.S. popularity in the early aughts, you could always find a bag of it sitting in our pantry, a loyal soldier waiting to be deployed. And that deployment is usually in the service of stretching out the odds and ends of a late-week vegetable drawer, no matter what the season. Here, I've paired it with winter root vegetables—I love how quinoa's nuttiness plays with the sweetness of the bold, colorful cabbage, carrots, and beets.

2 large carrots, trimmed and cut into 1-inch pieces

½ small head napa or green cabbage, cored and sliced into ¼-inch-thick pieces

2 tablespoons extra-virgin olive oil

1 tablespoon maple syrup

Kosher salt and freshly ground black pepper to taste

5 or 6 small beets, any color, scrubbed and ends trimmed (or store-bought, precooked beets), about 2 cups, chopped

1 cup uncooked quinoa

1 tablespoon unsalted butter

1 cup crumbled feta cheese

¼ cup toasted pistachios

1 bunch scallions, light green and white parts only, minced (about ⅔ cup)

4 small radishes, thinly sliced

⅔ cup All-Purpose Vinaigrette (page 217)

2 tablespoons chopped fresh chives

2 tablespoons chopped fresh flat-leaf parsley

Preheat the oven to 400°F. Line a sheet pan with foil.

On the prepared pan, combine the carrots, cabbage, olive oil, maple syrup, and some salt and pepper. If you aren't using store-bought beets, wrap the fresh beets together in a piece of foil and place them on one side of the sheet pan. Roast the vegetables until the carrots are golden and caramelized and the cabbage is lacquered but not too dark, about 25 minutes. Keep the beets in the oven until a knife easily slips through one, 20 to 30 minutes more. Open the foil packets to allow the beets to cool, then peel and quarter them. (If your beets are well cooked, the skins should slip off easily.)

Meanwhile, bring 2 cups water to a boil in a medium pot. Add the quinoa, stir, and cover with a tight-fitting lid. Reduce the heat and cook until all of the water has been absorbed, 13 to 15 minutes. Uncover, fluff with a fork, and transfer to a large bowl. Stir in the butter right away. Let cool.

To the large bowl with the cooled quinoa, add the beets, carrots, cabbage (it's OK if the chunks break into pieces), feta, pistachios, scallions, radishes, and vinaigrette and toss well. Top with the herbs and season with salt and pepper before serving.

*To veganize* / OMIT THE FETA AND BUTTER.

# WHEAT BERRIES *with* CRISPY TOFU, GRAPES, ARUGULA & FETA

Twice a week I brave the hour-and-a-half commute from the suburbs of New York to Brooklyn to work at Cup of Jo, the lifestyle website run by enthusiast extraordinaire Joanna Goddard. I look forward to these days for the camaraderie and creative collaboration, etc., etc., but also because her office is in Boerum Hill, with access to the kind of coffee and take-out food that just doesn't exist where I live. Even the chains are better: When plant-based Honeygrow (a Northeast DIY salad chain) opened up a few blocks away, I became obsessed with a magical combination of firm-but-tender wheat berries, sweet grapes, salty feta, and spicy nuts. I ate the salad so often my office mates started ordering it, too, calling it "The Jenny Salad." I talked about it so much that I ended up creating a—dare I say—even *better* version for my family back in the burbs. I always make extra so I have leftovers for lunch.

SERVES 4

62

bowls & salads

### HONEY-GINGER VINAIGRETTE

1 tablespoon honey

¼ cup white balsamic vinegar

¼ teaspoon ground ginger, or 1 teaspoon finely grated peeled fresh ginger

Kosher salt and freshly ground black pepper to taste

⅓ cup extra-virgin olive oil

1 cup uncooked wheat berries

Kosher salt

1 (14- to 15-ounce) block extra-firm tofu, pressed, drained, and cut into ½-inch cubes (see page 237)

3 tablespoons extra-virgin olive oil

2 tablespoons soy sauce

1 tablespoon cornstarch

3 cups arugula

1 cup crumbled feta

**MAKE THE DRESSING:** In a small jar or measuring cup, combine the honey, vinegar, ginger, salt, and pepper. (Note: If you don't have white balsamic, use white wine vinegar with a splash of regular balsamic. But don't fully swap in regular balsamic, which will be too overwhelming.) Cover the jar and shake vigorously to combine, or whisk the ingredients together thoroughly in the bowl. Add the olive oil and shake (or whisk) again until it is creamy and emulsified. Set aside until ready to use. Keeps in the refrigerator for up to 2 weeks.

Preheat the oven to 425°F. Line a sheet pan with parchment paper.

Add the wheat berries to a medium pot, covering them with water by 2 inches. Add some salt and simmer, stirring every 6 to 8 minutes, until the grains are tender, not tough. The cook time varies and can take up to 1 hour for the grains to become tender; I always start checking after 30 minutes. Drain the wheat berries in a colander and rinse under cold water, then drain again. Transfer them to a large bowl.

1 cup halved red seedless grapes

1 medium carrot, shaved into ribbons with a vegetable peeler

1 bunch scallions, white and light green parts only, minced (about ⅔ cup)

¼ cup whole shelled pistachios (I often throw in store-bought cayenne-spiked pistachios; look for the Wonderful brand)

While the wheat berries are cooking, toss the tofu with the olive oil, soy sauce, and cornstarch. Place the tofu on the prepared sheet pan and bake until golden and crispy around the edges, about 20 minutes. Remove from the oven and set aside to cool.

Add the cooled tofu to the wheat berries, then toss in the arugula, feta, grapes, carrot, scallions, pistachios, and vinaigrette and serve.

FOR THE
*holdout* / TOSS IN COOKED CHICKEN.

To *vegarize* / OMIT THE FETA AND REPLACE THE HONEY-GINGER VINAIGRETTE WITH ALL-PURPOSE VINAIGRETTE, PAGE 217.

# CABBAGE-KALE-TOFU SALAD
## with CITRUSY GINGER DRESSING

We've been making a version of this salad with shrimp or shredded chicken for as long as I can remember—usually in the beginning of the week when we feel like we need to redeem ourselves after excessive weekend indulging. This vegan take is every bit as satisfying and, like its non-vegan cousin, can be prepared up to a day in advance if you're making it for dinner guests. If you do that, just hold off on adding the avocado and tossing it with the dressing until about 15 minutes before serving.

1 (14- to 15-ounce) block extra-firm tofu, pressed, drained, and cut into ½-inch cubes (see page 237)

3 tablespoons grapeseed oil (or extra-virgin olive oil in a pinch)

2 tablespoons soy sauce

1 tablespoon cornstarch

5 cups shredded red cabbage (from a small cabbage)

2 cups shredded lacinato or curly kale

½ cup salted peanuts, chopped

3 tablespoons finely minced red onion or scallions (white and light green parts only)

½ cup fresh cilantro, chopped

1 avocado, halved, peeled, pitted, and cubed

2 tablespoons toasted sesame seeds (optional)

### CITRUSY GINGER DRESSING

2 teaspoons Dijon mustard

¼ cup fresh orange juice

1 tablespoon fresh lime juice

1 tablespoon soy sauce

2 teaspoons minced fresh ginger

½ teaspoon sriracha sauce

⅓ cup extra-virgin olive oil

¼ teaspoon toasted sesame oil

Preheat the oven to 425°F. Line a sheet pan with parchment paper.

In a medium bowl, toss the tofu with the grapeseed oil, soy sauce, and cornstarch. Transfer the tofu to the prepared sheet pan and roast until brown and crispy around the edges, about 20 minutes. Remove from the oven and set aside to cool.

**WHILE THE TOFU ROASTS, MAKE THE DRESSING:** In a small bowl, whisk together the mustard, orange juice, lime juice, soy sauce, ginger, sriracha, olive oil, and sesame oil.

In a large serving bowl, combine the cabbage, kale, peanuts, red onion, cilantro, avocado, and sesame seeds (if using). Add the cooled tofu along with the dressing and toss to coat.

*FOR THE* **holdout**

*vegan*

*TOSS IN COOKED SHRIMP OR CHICKEN WHERE NECESSARY.*

# PIZZA SALAD *with* WHITE BEANS

This recipe was born of my desire to add protein to one of our family's favorite vegetarian dinners: salad pizza, where you top a tomato pizza with an Italian-dressing-dressed salad; see page 40. One night, I served salad pizza with a side dish of brothy white beans, storing both leftovers together in a container for lunch the next day. That next day was like a "Who Put His Chocolate in My Peanut Butter" moment—I couldn't believe how well the salad and the beans melded together. If you have thought to marinate your beans a few hours ahead of time, you will appreciate their deeper flavor in this salad. However, even if you just let the beans swim in olive oil, red wine vinegar, and some fresh herbs for 15 minutes (roughly as long as it takes to assemble the rest of this), you'll be satisfied with the results. And it goes without saying that this salad is particularly welcome in August and September, when tomatoes are peaking and warm summer days call for minimally invasive cooking.

3 cups Marinated
Beans (page 163)

1 large bunch Bibb
or Little Gem lettuce, torn
(about 8 cups)

2 cups quartered or sliced
tomatoes, preferably grape or
fresh, ripe, and sweet heirlooms

2 tablespoons finely minced
red onion

1 cup halved bocconcini
(small mozzarella balls) or
½-inch cubes fresh mozzarella

8 large fresh basil leaves,
chopped

¼ cup grated Parmesan cheese

Hand-Torn Croutons (page 226)
(optional)

If you haven't already, prepare the marinated beans and let them sit at least 15 minutes.

In a large shallow bowl, toss the lettuce, tomatoes, onion, bocconcini, basil, and Parmesan. Toss in the beans with their marinade and croutons (if using) and serve.

*To* **Vegarize** / OMIT THE MOZZARELLA AND PARM.

*For The* **holdout** / ADD CHOPPED SALAMI OR PROSCIUTTO.

# CHICKPEA CAESAR SALAD

In the course of writing this book, Abby would repeatedly ask me, "You wrote somewhere it was Chickpea Caesar Salad that convinced me I could be a vegetarian, right?" (*Yes, Abby.*) It was indeed her idea to swap out the chicken in Caesar salad for crispy chickpeas, and I have to say, it was a pretty great one. She is fond of saying she prefers this dinner to a burger any day of the week. ("Did you write the line about the burger, Mom?" *Yes, Abby.*) This is another example of a recipe that can be as simple or as complicated as you have time for—it's optimal and amazing when all the ingredients are homemade, of course, but the salad still works when you cut corners with any of the ingredients' store-bought companions (packaged crispy chickpeas, store-bought croutons). I'd say, on average, it makes an appearance on our table at least once a week. Sometimes we add Seven-Minute Eggs (page 197) for good measure.

2 heads romaine lettuce, torn or chopped into 1-inch pieces

2 cups cherry tomatoes, sliced

2 tablespoons finely minced red onion or scallions (white and light green parts only)

3 cups Crispy Chickpeas (page 198)

Caesar Dressing (page 204)

1 cup Hand-Torn Croutons (page 226)

*SERVING*

4 Seven-Minute Eggs (page 197), halved (optional)

Freshly grated Parmesan cheese

*To* **Veganize**

SWAP OUT CAESAR DRESSING FOR NO-BLENDER VEGAN CAESAR DRESSING, PAGE 205; OMIT EGGS AND PARM.

Combine the romaine, tomatoes, red onion, chickpeas, dressing, and croutons in a giant salad bowl and serve topped with egg halves (if using) and Parmesan.

**ALTERNATE METHOD**
## Broiled Caesar Salad with Chickpeas

*No matter how much you or your kids might love a classic Caesar, the flavorless romaine situation in the dead of winter can make it a pretty grim proposition. That changed for us, though, once we discovered this broiling method for romaine hearts. When halved and "basted" with the dressing, they come to life— sweet and roasty on the top, cool and crunchy on the bottom, and in-between crevices filled with the salty- tangy bites.*

*Here's the how-to: Arrange an oven rack in the top position and preheat the broiler. Place 8 romaine halves (cut lengthwise from 4 romaine hearts, with the main stem intact), cut-side up, on a sheet pan. Brush each one generously with a few swipes of Caesar Dressing and sprinkle with a little Parmesan. Broil until the tops look shriveled and browned but not burned, about 5 minutes. Using tongs, transfer the romaine to a platter. Top with your crispy chickpeas, red onion, and herbs and drizzle everything with more dressing. We've made this with Herby Buttermilk Ranch (page 216), too.*

# STRAWBERRY-FETA SALAD *with* BEETS & BEANS

What makes this salad special is how much is happening in every bite: sweet-tangy strawberries, creamy-salty feta, and rich crunchy nuts. You don't need me to tell you that it will look and taste amazing when the beets are fresh and in-season, during that time of year when you can swing by the farmers' market and pick up a few bunches in all their multicolored glory—candy-striped, golden, red, purple. But life doesn't always work out that way, and it's nice to know that you can still enjoy a version of this salad on a weeknight when you're just swinging by the dinky market in the strip mall that sells the precooked beets. If you do that, this dinner is a strict assembly job (my favorite kind of dinner) and will take under 10 minutes to come together.

**1 pound medium beets (about 5), any color, scrubbed and trimmed, or 2 cups precooked whole beets (about 10 ounces), sliced into coin-size pieces**

**2 tablespoons extra-virgin olive oil**

**1 tablespoon red wine vinegar**

**Kosher salt and freshly ground black pepper to taste**

**1 large head Bibb lettuce, torn into pieces (8 cups)**

**1½ cups strawberries, washed, hulled, and sliced**

**1½ cups cooked gigante beans (or butter beans) or 1 (15-ounce) can, rinsed and drained**

**1 cup crumbled feta cheese (about 4 ounces)**

**⅓ cup crushed pistachios (see page 237)**

**3 tablespoons roughly chopped or torn fresh mint (from about 12 leaves)**

**1 bunch scallions (white and light green parts only), minced**

**⅔ cup All-Purpose Vinaigrette (page 217; use white balsamic vinegar)**

Preheat the oven to 375°F.

If roasting your own beets (skip to the next step if you are using store-bought, precooked beets): Wrap the fresh beets in foil and bake for 1 hour 30 minutes. Remove them from the oven, carefully unwrap the foil (the steam will be *very* hot), and let the beets cool. Once they are cool enough to handle, remove the skin using your hands. (If your beets are fully cooked, the skins should slip off easily.)

Slice home-cooked or precooked beets into small chunks or coin-size pieces and toss them in a small bowl with the olive oil, the red wine vinegar, salt, and pepper.

In a large bowl, combine the lettuce, strawberries, beans, feta, pistachios, mint, scallions, and beets. Season all over with salt and pepper, then toss gently with the vinaigrette.

# soups

# CHILLED ASPARAGUS SOUP
## with CROUTONS & CHIVES

This is sort of like asparagus gazpacho and is the most delicious when (a) asparagus is in season, (b) it's a warm night, and (c) you pile on the garnishes, like homemade sourdough croutons and crispy fresh sprouts. It's best after being chilled in the refrigerator for at least 1 hour, but I've had it at room temperature, too, and I wouldn't send it back.

2 bunches asparagus (2 pounds), woody ends trimmed

2 tablespoons Dijon mustard

½ cup extra-virgin olive oil, plus more (optional) for drizzling

Kosher salt and freshly ground black pepper to taste

1 tablespoon fresh lemon juice (from ½ small lemon)

¾ cup vegetable stock, store-bought or homemade (page 232)

### SERVING

Chopped fresh chives

Hand-Torn Croutons (page 226; swap in sourdough bread if possible)

Plain yogurt (omit for vegans)

Pea shoots or arugula sprouts

Chili oil (optional)

Prepare an ice bath by filling a large bowl with ice and water; set aside.

Fill a deep skillet or a large pot with water and bring it to a boil over high heat. Add the asparagus, decreasing the heat slightly until it's at a low boil. Simmer until cooked through, 4 to 5 minutes. Using tongs, remove the asparagus from the skillet and immediately plunge it into the ice bath to stop further cooking and retain the bright green color. Leave the asparagus cooking liquid in the skillet.

Chop the asparagus into thirds and add it to a blender with the mustard, olive oil, salt, pepper, lemon juice, stock, and a tablespoon of the asparagus cooking water. Blend, adding a few tablespoons of cooking liquid as needed, until the soup reaches your desired consistency. If you have time, cover and chill it in the refrigerator for at least 1 hour and up to 1 day.

When ready to eat, divide the soup evenly among the bowls and serve with your desired toppings.

/ vegan /

# STEWY BLACK LENTILS *with* CHARD & FETA

This somewhere-between-a-soup-and-a-stew will 100 percent work with the regular old (delicious) brown lentils that you can find in any supermarket. I love black lentils, though, because they retain their firmness more and are so pretty! (They're called beluga lentils because they look like beluga caviar.) Make sure to add the chard at the last minute so it stays vibrant and green.

3 tablespoons extra-virgin olive oil

½ small yellow onion, finely chopped

2 small carrots, chopped (about ¾ cup)

1 celery stalk, chopped (about ⅓ cup)

Kosher salt and freshly ground black pepper to taste

2 tablespoons harissa paste

16 ounces brown or black (beluga) lentils, rinsed and drained

About 6 cups vegetable stock, store-bought or homemade (page 232)

2 fresh thyme sprigs, plus more for garnish

4 cups loosely packed roughly chopped Swiss chard (including stems)

### SERVING

3 to 4 ounces feta, crumbled (about 1 cup)

Fresh dill, chopped

4 generous dollops plain Greek yogurt

Za'atar Pizza Dough Flatbread (page 220) or crusty bread

In a large stockpot, warm the olive oil over medium heat. Add the onion, carrots, celery, salt, and pepper and cook until softened, stirring occasionally, about 5 minutes. Stir in harissa and cook another minute so it gets a little toasty.

Add the lentils, stirring until they glisten, then add the stock and thyme. Increase the heat and bring the stock to a boil, then lower it to a simmer, adding more water as it cooks so it covers the lentils by about an inch. Cook until the lentils are tender but still hold their shape, about 20 minutes.

Turn the heat to low and remove the thyme sprigs. I like the consistency to be a little chunky, but if you like it soupier, by all means add a bit more stock or water at this point to loosen it up.

Stir in the chard, and cook until it wilts, another 1 to 2 minutes. Serve in bowls with the feta, dill, thyme leaves, dollops of yogurt, and bread.

To vegarize / OMIT THE FETA AND YOGURT.

# EASIEST WHITE BEAN SOUP *with*

### (A) GIGANTIC CROUTONS, (B) KALE PESTO, (C) BROILED SCALLIONS, OR (D) ALL OF THE ABOVE

As with many soups, this one is about the add-ons. Serving it with the three suggested toppings (croutons, pesto, scallions) will take this to the next level, but you're still OK if you only have the time or sanity for the first two. Tip for parents serving soup skeptics: The kids might think of the soup as more of a "dip" if you serve it in a small bowl and the crouton like a piece of toast on the side.

5 tablespoons extra-virgin olive oil, plus more for drizzling

½ small yellow onion, finely chopped

Kosher salt and freshly ground black pepper to taste

Pinch of dried red pepper flakes

2 garlic cloves, minced

4½ cups cooked cannellini beans, or 3 (15-ounce) cans, rinsed and drained

2½ to 3 cups vegetable stock, store-bought or homemade (page 232)

2 tablespoons sherry vinegar

4 thick-cut slices crusty bread, such as ciabatta

4 tablespoons grated Parmesan cheese (about 1 ounce)

### SERVING (OPTIONAL)

Kale Pesto (page 206) or your favorite store-bought pesto

Broiled scallions (toss one bunch trimmed scallions, with stems, in 2 tablespoons olive oil, place on a foil-lined sheet pan, and broil for 5 minutes; let cool and roughly chop)

Chopped fresh chives

*To vegarize*

OMIT THE PARM AND TOP WITH STORE-BOUGHT VEGAN BASIL PESTO.

In a stockpot set over low heat, combine 3 tablespoons of the olive oil, the onion, salt, black pepper, and red pepper flakes. Sauté until the onion is golden and slightly caramelized, stirring often, for as long as you have patience, but a minimum of 5 to 7 minutes. (A lot of the depth in this soup will come from caramelizing the onion, so the longer, the better.) Add the garlic and cook until fragrant, about 2 minutes. Add the beans and just enough stock to cover. Increase the heat to medium-high and bring the mixture to an aggressive simmer until warmed through, about 3 minutes.

Remove the pot from the heat and, using a slotted spoon, scoop out and set aside about 1 cup of the beans. Stir the vinegar into the pot, then puree the soup using a handheld immersion blender. Set back on the stove top over low heat to keep warm.

Preheat the broiler. Place the bread slices on a sheet pan and broil on the top rack of the oven just until toasted but not quite golden, about 1½ minutes. (Watch carefully so they don't burn.) Flip them over, brush with the remaining 2 tablespoons olive oil, sprinkle each with 1 tablespoon Parmesan, and broil until the cheese has melted, another 1½ minutes. Remove from the oven.

Serve the soup in large shallow bowls, placing one giant crouton in the middle of the soup along with a few reserved beans, the pesto, scallions, and chives, if using. Drizzle with more olive oil just before serving.

# BUTTERNUT SQUASH SOUP
## with COCONUT MILK & LIME

You're probably thinking, *I already have a recipe for butternut squash soup,* but let me assure you: you have room for one more. I love when a veganized recipe becomes better than my original (which used butter and chicken broth). This coconutty-lime version has so much going on—in the best possible way. If you want to make it more substantive, serve with toasted naan or a scoop of white or basmati rice.

1 tablespoon coconut oil

2 tablespoons olive oil

1 medium yellow onion, finely chopped

1 tablespoon curry powder

Pinch of cayenne pepper

Kosher salt and freshly ground black pepper to taste

6 cups cubed butternut squash (from 2 to 2½ pounds squash)

3½ cups vegetable stock, store-bought or homemade (page 232)

½ cup coconut milk (any kind)

### SERVING

Lime zest

Toasted coconut flakes

Chopped fresh basil

Combine the coconut oil and olive oil in a medium stockpot set over medium-low heat. When the coconut oil liquefies, increase the heat to medium and add the onion, curry powder, cayenne, salt, and black pepper. Cook until the onion is soft and the spices are toasty, about 5 minutes.

Add the squash and stock (the squash should be just barely submerged; add water as necessary) and bring to a boil. Reduce the heat and simmer until the squash is very thoroughly cooked and almost mushy, 15 to 20 minutes. Remove from the heat and, using a handheld immersion blender, whirl the soup until it is pureed and very smooth. (If you don't have an immersion blender, you can do this in a regular blender, but just make sure the soup has cooled significantly before you puree, or puree it in batches.) It's OK if the soup is a little thicker than you prefer. Remove from the heat and stir in the coconut milk. If it's still too thick, stir in water, a tablespoon at a time, until it reaches your preferred consistency.

Serve with toppings.

/ vegan /

# pastas & noodles

# RIGATONI *with* HONEYNUT SQUASH, CHARD & HAZELNUTS

Honeynut squash is like a butternut squash's best version of itself—sweeter and more intensely flavored. This recipe—which essentially adds vegetables to a peppery *cacio e pepe*–style sauce—is a simple, healthy, warm-your-bones way to enjoy it. Butternut or kabocha squash would be a fine swap-in, and the pre-cubed varieties you can find in most produce aisles are your weeknight self's best friend.

Kosher salt to taste

2 small honeynut squashes (about 3 pounds total), peeled, halved, seeded, and cut into ½-inch cubes (6 to 7 cups)

1 small onion, roughly chopped

4 tablespoons extra-virgin olive oil

½ teaspoon dried red pepper flakes

Freshly ground black pepper to taste

1 pound rigatoni or tube pasta of your choice—just don't use noodles

3 tablespoons unsalted butter

1 garlic clove, minced

5 cups roughly chopped Swiss chard (including stems), amaranth, kale, or spinach

½ cup shredded Parmesan cheese (about 2 ounces)

⅓ cup crushed or roughly chopped toasted hazelnuts (see page 237 for crushing tips)

Preheat the oven to 425°F. Line a sheet pan with parchment paper. Bring a large pot of salted water to a boil.

Combine the squash and onion on the prepared sheet pan and drizzle with 3 tablespoons of the olive oil. Sprinkle with red pepper flakes, salt, and black pepper and, using your hands, toss until every piece is coated and shiny. Roast until the squash looks crispy around the edges, 20 to 25 minutes.

Meanwhile, when the salted water comes to a boil, cook the rigatoni according to the package directions until it's al dente. Reserve about ½ cup of the pasta water, then drain the pasta and immediately toss it right in the strainer with 1 tablespoon of the butter.

Set the pasta pot back on the stovetop over low heat. Add the remaining 2 tablespoons butter, the remaining 1 tablespoon olive oil, and the garlic. Cook until the garlic is golden, about 1 minute, then add the chard, salt, and black pepper, tossing until the chard has softened and wilted, about 2 minutes. Toss in the rigatoni along with the Parmesan, more salt and black pepper, and about ¼ cup of the reserved pasta water to help distribute the cheese and make the pasta saucy. (Add more pasta water, a tablespoon at a time, as needed.) Toss in the squash-onion mixture, then serve in bowls topped with hazelnuts.

# TAGLIATELLE *with* CORN, TOMATOES, "ONION-BACON" & BASIL

Over the years, we've made this pasta with shrimp, with bacon, and with both shrimp and bacon, and, when the tomatoes and corn are at peak sweetness, it practically shouts summer. Which is to say, it's easy, fresh, and hits notes that you can get only a few weeks a year. I worried about making an entirely plant-based version of it, but then I learned a trick from *Bon Appétit*'s Chris Morocco: If you caramelize red onions at a low heat (for about as long as it takes to boil water and then cook the pasta), they take on a richness that rivals bacon. Add that to late August corn and tomatoes, and you've got a surefire crowd-pleaser.

Kosher salt to taste

1 medium red onion, sliced

4 tablespoons extra-virgin olive oil

16 ounces tagliatelle or spaghetti (like the dish on the cover)

3 tablespoons unsalted butter

1 garlic clove, minced

Freshly ground black pepper to taste

Pinch of dried red pepper flakes

4 cups corn kernels (from about 4 medium ears)

3 to 3½ cups roughly chopped ripe tomatoes (from about 3 medium tomatoes) and their juices

½ cup freshly grated Parmesan cheese (about 2 ounces)

4 fresh basil leaves, chopped

Bring a large pot of salted water to a boil.

In a separate large pot or Dutch oven set over medium-low heat, combine the onion and 3 tablespoons of the olive oil and stir every few minutes.

Cook the tagliatelle in the boiling water according to the package directions. When the pasta is just about done, reserve 1 cup of the pasta water, then drain the pasta and toss it right in the strainer with the remaining 1 tablespoon olive oil to prevent sticking.

Add the butter to the red onion, which should be caramelly and slightly shriveled by this point, along with the garlic, salt, black pepper, and red pepper flakes. Cook for another minute. Add the corn and tomatoes and cook until the vegetables release a lot of liquid, another 4 to 5 minutes. It should look like a bright, chunky sauce.

Add the pasta and Parmesan to the vegetables, tossing to distribute and coat the pasta with the sauce. Add a drizzle of pasta water as needed to help the cheese distribute evenly. Top with basil and serve.

# CHICKPEA-PASTA MAC & CHEESE
## with CHOPPED TOMATOES

Sometimes, when I want a nice, easy sell at the dinner table without feeling like we're going full-on carb-fest, I replace regular shells in our mac and cheese with chickpea-flour pasta (a single serving of chickpea pasta contains as much nutritional value and protein as a whole can of chickpeas), and I top it with a chopped tomato salad that helps cut the richness. For the longest time, homemade mac and cheese was not something I felt like whipping up on a weeknight, but most of the reason for that was that I had a hard time getting over the hurdle of making the béchamel base, the buttery-flour sauce that lends a rich creaminess to the dish. Like most things in cooking, though, as soon as you do it once or twice, you realize it ain't exactly splitting the atom here—in fact, it couldn't be easier. Also, though this recipe calls for 1½ cups of cheddar and another cup of Parm, I often find myself tossing in scraps of leftover cheese (Jack, Gruyère, or whatever else is in the fridge) to get to the 2½-cup mark, so you can experiment a little there. Also also! I make this all the time when families come over for dinner; it's a great side dish for grown-ups, and I can count on most kids being pretty pumped about seeing it on the spread.

Kosher salt to taste

4 tablespoons (½ stick) unsalted butter, plus more for greasing

16 ounces chickpea pasta shells

¼ cup all-purpose flour

3 cups whole milk

¼ teaspoon Worcestershire sauce

Freshly ground black pepper to taste

½ teaspoon garlic powder

6 ounces sharp cheddar cheese, shredded (about 1½ cups)

2½ ounces grated Parmigiano-Reggiano (about 1 cup)

½ cup panko bread crumbs

2 tablespoons extra-virgin olive oil

Bring a large pot of salted water to a boil.

Preheat the oven to 425°F. Grease a 13 × 9-inch baking dish with a little butter.

Cook the pasta in the boiling water according to the package directions until it's al dente, about 7 minutes. Drain and set aside. Return the pot to the stovetop, add the butter, and melt it over medium-low heat. Once it's melted, stir in the flour, whisking constantly until it becomes golden, 1 to 2 minutes. In a large measuring cup or a bowl (but I like something with a spout), combine the milk, Worcestershire, salt, pepper, and garlic powder. Gradually whisk the liquid into the pot—it's important to add the liquid slowly to avoid clumps. Turn the heat to medium and whisk until the béchamel is thick and saucy, 6 to 8 minutes. Remove from the heat.

CONTINUES

2 cups chopped fresh tomatoes (any kind)

1 small garlic clove, pressed

1 tablespoon red wine vinegar

Leaves from 3 fresh thyme sprigs

Kosher salt and freshly ground pepper to taste

To the béchamel in the pot, add the pasta, cheddar, and ¾ cup of the Parm and stir to combine. It's OK if it seems liquidy—that liquid will be absorbed in the baking. Transfer the pasta to the prepared baking dish.

In a small bowl, use a fork to mix together the remaining Parm and the panko, salt, pepper, and olive oil. Sprinkle this on top of the pasta and bake until it is bubbly and the topping is golden brown, 20 to 25 minutes.

**WHILE THE PASTA IS BAKING, PREPARE THE CHOPPED TOMATOES:** In a small bowl, combine the tomatoes, garlic, red wine vinegar, thyme, salt, and pepper.

Serve each helping of mac and cheese with a few spoonfuls of chopped tomatoes.

*pastas & noodles*

# THE GREENEST PASTA (SPAGHETTI with PEAS, BROCCOLINI & KALE PESTO)

I love a pasta dinner where you can make the sauce in about the same amount of time as it takes to prepare the noodles. If you are missing a protein hit, this pairs well with quick Marinated Beans (page 163).

Kosher salt to taste

16 ounces spaghetti
(or ribbon-shaped noodles,
like tagliatelle)

½ cup frozen peas (they don't
have to be thawed)

1 pound Broccolini, trimmed
and chopped into 2-inch pieces

2 tablespoons unsalted butter

¾ cup Kale Pesto (page 206)
or store-bought basil pesto

### SERVING

Grated Parmesan cheese

Freshly ground black pepper
to taste

Bring a large pot of salted water to a boil. Cook the pasta according to the package directions until it's al dente. About 2 minutes before you drain the pasta, add the peas and Broccolini to the pasta pot. Reserve ½ cup of the pasta water, then drain the pasta, peas, and Broccolini in a strainer. Add the butter to everything in the strainer and toss well.

Return the pot to the stovetop (without heat) and add the pesto. Slowly whisk in the reserved ½ cup pasta water until the pesto is thinned but not brothy (it should coat your spoon). Add the spaghetti and vegetables and toss until the pesto is well distributed. Serve with grated Parm and a few twists of freshly ground black pepper.

# tacos, tortillas & enchiladas

# MIGAS TACOS

The first time I had *migas*, it was not so much a choice as it was a command. I was in Austin on a work trip, and when I asked the waiter at a restaurant in South Austin where I should have lunch the next day, he pulled a paper napkin off my table and drew a map with a big black *X* on the corner of Cesar Chavez and Chicon. "Veracruz," he wrote. "Best tacos ever! Order the migas taco on corn!" Anyone who has ever been to Austin—famous for its migas—knows the strange and magical chemistry that happens when you take five seemingly basic ingredients (eggs, cheddar, jalapeños, tortilla chips, onions), cook them low and slow, then stuff it all inside a soft corn tortilla with hot sauce. They were otherworldly—the tender eggs, the fresh tortillas, the deep blue sky canopied over my picnic table. Though I'll never replicate them at home exactly, I like to think this version comes close. Note: This is an excellent use for those crumbled tortilla chip shards at the bottom of the bag.

8 (6-inch) corn tortillas

2 tablespoons unsalted butter

½ small yellow onion, finely chopped

1 large jalapeño pepper, stemmed, seeded, and ribs removed, minced (about 3 tablespoons)

Kosher salt and freshly ground black pepper to taste

10 large eggs

1 cup crumbled tortilla chips

⅔ cup shredded Monterey Jack cheese

### SERVING

Salsa Fresca (page 209) or store-bought salsa

1 avocado, halved, pitted, peeled, and sliced

½ cup chopped fresh cilantro

Hot sauce or Tomatillo Sauce (page 203)

Lime wedges

Preheat the oven to 300°F.

Wrap the tortillas in foil and place them in the oven, for at least 5 minutes and up to 15 minutes.

Set a large nonstick or cast-iron skillet over medium-low heat. Add the butter and, once it melts, stir in the onion, jalapeño, and some salt and pepper. When the vegetables are soft, after 2 minutes, spread them out evenly across the surface of the pan. Reduce the heat to low.

In a medium mixing bowl, whisk together the eggs, tortilla chips, cheese, salt, and pepper. Pour the egg mixture over the onion mixture and stir gently until the eggs are cooked but still tender (or until scrambled to your liking). Remove the tortillas from the oven and unwrap them. Distribute the eggs evenly among the tortillas and top with Salsa Fresca, avocado slices, and cilantro. Serve with hot sauce and lime.

# REFRIED BLACK BEAN TOSTADAS
## *with* AVOCADO & PICKLED ONIONS

We live in a suburb of New York City, so almost as soon as my daughters were old enough to get themselves on the commuter train, they were navigating the city on their own. It was important to me that they knew how to read a subway map, hail a cab, and walk through Midtown without being taken for tourists, but they had different priorities. They just wanted to find good food, preferably cheap and Instagrammable. I was fine with that, too, especially since they came home begging me to re-create the refried black bean tostadas they had at Tacombi, a popular Mexican spot with locations all around Manhattan. It wasn't hard for me to oblige. These show up on our dinner table a *lot*, especially since they are a cinch to assemble.

**4 tablespoons neutral oil (such as vegetable or canola), plus more as needed**

**8 (6-inch) corn tortillas**

**½ small yellow onion, finely chopped**

**1 medium garlic clove, halved**

**1 teaspoon ground cumin**

**Kosher salt and freshly ground black pepper to taste**

**3 cups cooked black beans, or 2 (15-ounce) cans, rinsed and drained**

**1 avocado, halved, pitted, peeled, and sliced**

**1 cup Pickled Onions (page 231)**

**Queso fresco**

**Chopped fresh cilantro**

### SERVING

**Lime wedges**

**Hot sauce**

Heat 2 tablespoons of the oil in a medium cast-iron skillet set over medium-high heat until it is hot, about 5 minutes. Fry the tortillas, one at a time, until they look crispy and golden, about 1 minute total, turning them halfway through, adding more oil as needed while you continue to fry the remaining tortillas. Drain the tortillas on a paper-towel-lined plate as you go.

When all of the tortillas are fried, decrease the heat to medium-low, wipe out any excess oil (you want a thin coat), and add the onion, garlic (cut-side down), cumin, and some salt and pepper. After about 1 minute, remove the garlic halves from the oil. Mix in the beans and ⅓ cup water and mash everything with a fork until the beans are heated through. (Alternately, you could save time by starting this process in another skillet while the tortillas are frying, but if the clock's not ticking, I'd rather have one less big-ticket item to wash at the end of the night.)

To assemble the tostadas, spread a layer of beans on each tortilla. Top each with the avocado, pickled onions, queso fresco, and cilantro. Serve with a lime wedge and hot sauce.

*To vegarize* / SKIP THE QUESO FRESCO.

# ROASTED BUTTERNUT SQUASH & BLACK BEAN TACOS

I know what you're thinking: *Are we at Taco Bell with those hard-shell tacos?* The truth is, when I know the filling is going to be a tough sell, sometimes I focus on the container instead, and in this case, the taco shell—basically a giant salty, crispy tortilla chip—is as appealing a container as there ever was, especially when contrasted with the soft, sweet filling. I often heat up a combination of both hard and soft and let the diners decide what they want at the table. You can find a pretty decent selection of organic brand hard shells in most major supermarkets. Note: These are amazing with Cilantro Pesto (page 206), but if you can't swing that on a weeknight, a squeeze of lime juice and cilantro will certainly suffice as a topping.

1 small butternut squash (1½ to 2 pounds), peeled, seeded, and cut into ½-inch chunks, or 18 to 20 ounces store-bought pre-peeled and pre-chopped squash, cut into ½-inch chunks (about 4 cups total)

4 tablespoons extra-virgin olive oil

¾ teaspoon smoked paprika

Kosher salt and freshly ground black pepper to taste

8 (6-inch) soft corn tortillas, hard taco shells, or a mix of both

2 garlic cloves, finely chopped

½ teaspoon ground cumin

2 tablespoons canned chopped mild green chiles

3 cups cooked black beans, or 2 (15-ounce) cans, rinsed and drained

6 scallions, white and light green parts only, minced

### SERVING (OPTIONAL)

Cilantro Pesto (page 206)

Sliced radishes

Lime wedges

Preheat the oven to 425°F. Line a sheet pan with foil.

On the prepared sheet pan, combine the squash, 2 tablespoons of the olive oil, the paprika, salt, and pepper. Toss to coat the squash with the oil and spices (I use my hands; then I have two fewer things—a mixing bowl and a wooden spoon—to wash later). Roast until the squash is crispy and golden on the corners, 20 to 25 minutes. Remove from the oven and decrease the heat to 300°F. Wrap the tortillas (whether soft or hard) in foil and warm them for 10 minutes.

Meanwhile, heat the remaining 2 tablespoons olive oil in a skillet over medium heat until hot but not smoking. Add the garlic, cumin, salt, and pepper and cook, stirring, until the garlic is golden, about 1 minute. Stir in the chiles, then the beans, coarsely mashing them with a large fork until combined. Add ⅓ cup water and the scallions and cook, stirring often, until most of the water is absorbed, about 5 minutes. Remove from the heat.

Stuff each tortilla with a few tablespoons of beans and a few pieces of squash. Top with a dollop of cilantro pesto and some sliced radishes and serve with lime wedges (if using).

*/ vegan /*

# TACOS *with* REFRIED PINTOS, CRISPY SHIITAKES & KALE

Andy scraped these together on one of those nights when it felt like we had no food in the house, and we've been making and improving on them ever since. We lean on mushrooms for their meaty consistency and deep umami, but this is doubly true for shiitake mushrooms. When you cook them long enough to release their liquid and get crispy, they taste like little bites of pork or beef. Note: The easiest way to warm tortillas is in an oven, wrapped in foil, as directed here, but if I have time, I prefer to cook them over a grate one by one with tongs on the stovetop.

8 (6-inch) corn tortillas

1 (14-ounce) can refried pinto beans

1 tablespoon canned chopped mild green chiles

3 tablespoons extra-virgin olive oil

2 cloves garlic, halved

Shake of dried red pepper flakes

4 cups sliced shiitake mushrooms (10 to 12 ounces)

Kosher salt and freshly ground black pepper to taste

3½ ounces kale (curly or Tuscan), stems removed, and roughly chopped (about 4 cups)

2 tablespoons red wine vinegar

### SERVING

Avocado slices

Chopped scallions, white and light green parts only

Lime wedges

Preheat the oven to 300°F.

Wrap the tortillas in foil and heat in the oven (for at least 10 minutes and up to 15) while you prepare the filling.

In a small saucepan set over low heat, heat the refried beans. Stir in the chiles, and keep warm over the lowest heat possible.

Meanwhile, heat the olive oil in a large skillet set over medium heat. Add the garlic halves, cut-side down, and cook for 2 minutes to infuse the oil, then remove. Add red pepper flakes to the pan. Stir in the mushrooms, salt, and pepper and cook until they release all their liquid, 8 to 10 minutes. Once they are shriveled and crispy looking, stir in the kale and cook until it wilts, about 2 minutes. Remove from the heat and stir in the vinegar.

Remove the tortillas from the oven. Spread each tortilla with refried beans, then top with the mushroom-kale mix, avocado slices, and scallions and serve with lime wedges.

/ vegan /

Andy and I both love to cook, but because my work schedule is way more flexible than his, I'm usually the one putting together something quick and easy on the weeknights, and, in general, he takes over on the weekend. So when Andy started making enchiladas for Sunday dinner—a frequent request from the kids—I figured it was one of those dreaded project recipes, something long and involved, a recipe that took at least two loops of his very comprehensive Wilco playlist. It certainly tasted like that kind of recipe. The truth is, I didn't ask many questions while I was reading on the couch and scrolling through Twitter. Once it became clear to me that these enchiladas were worthy of the new vegetarian canon, I asked him to walk me through the recipe while I took notes. Essentially, he said, it boils down to this: "Heat up a can of beans with a can of green chiles, stuff into tortillas, cover with sauce, and bake with cheese on top."

"That's it?" I asked.

"What did you think?" he replied. "They're enchiladas."

What did I think? I don't know. But it's true they're *that* easy. (The hardest part is making the sauce, which can be shortcut with store-bought, obviously.) So easy, I now even make them on weeknights and started playing around with the fillings and the sauce. Here are the two versions that appear most frequently on our table.

## Green Enchiladas with Tomatillo Sauce

2 tablespoons neutral oil (such as vegetable or canola), plus more for brushing the dish

1 garlic clove, minced

½ medium white onion, chopped (save the other half for the tomatillo sauce)

1 teaspoon ground cumin

Kosher salt and freshly ground black pepper to taste

2 cups cooked white beans, such as lima or great northern, or 1½ (15-ounce) cans, rinsed and drained

1 cup thawed frozen chopped spinach, squeezed dry

2 tablespoons canned diced green chiles

7 or 8 (6-inch) flour tortillas

1½ cups shredded sharp cheddar cheese, plus more for topping

2½ cups Tomatillo Sauce (page 203)

2 tablespoons minced red onion

### SERVING (OPTIONAL)

Crumbled queso fresco

Chopped fresh cilantro

Preheat the oven to 375°F.

Heat the oil in a large deep oven-proof skillet set over medium heat. Add the garlic, white onion, cumin, and some salt and pepper and cook, stirring occasionally, until the cumin gets toasty and aromatic, about 3 minutes. Add the beans, spinach, and green chiles, and cook until everything is warmed through, about 5 minutes. Mash the beans slightly with a fork or potato masher and drizzle in a little water to loosen the mixture if it's too pasty. (The spinach will probably have enough water to loosen it.)

CONTINUES

## Andy's Sunday*  Enchiladas with  Red Sauce

2 tablespoons neutral oil (such as vegetable or canola), plus more for brushing the dish

½ small yellow onion, chopped

1 large garlic clove, minced

Kosher salt and freshly ground black pepper to taste

3 cups cooked pinto beans, or 2 (15-ounce) cans, rinsed and drained

3 tablespoons canned chopped mild green Hatch chiles

½ teaspoon cumin

7 or 8 (6-inch) flour tortillas

2 cups shredded sharp cheddar cheese, plus more for topping

3 cups red enchilada sauce, store-bought or homemade (recipe opposite)

2 tablespoons minced red onion

*SERVING (OPTIONAL)*

Sour cream

Crumbled queso fresco

Avocado slices

Chopped fresh cilantro

Sliced radishes

Canned pickled jalapeño peppers

Salsa Fresca (page 209)

Brush a 13 × 9-inch baking dish with oil. Spread 2 to 3 tablespoons of the bean filling down the middle of each tortilla, then sprinkle a little shredded cheddar on top. Roll the tortilla around the filling and place it, seam-side down, in the prepared baking dish. Repeat with the cheese (you want to use about half the cheese here), remaining tortillas, and beans.

Smother the rolled tortillas with the tomatillo sauce, using the back of a spoon to make sure all the tortillas are covered with sauce, and top with the remaining cheese and red onion. Bake until the cheese is bubbly and golden, 15 to 20 minutes. Serve with your desired toppings.

Serves 4 to 6

*IN NAME ONLY. TOTALLY EASY ENOUGH FOR A WEEKNIGHT.

Preheat the oven to 375°F.

In a large deep skillet set over medium heat, combine the oil, the yellow onion, garlic, salt, and pepper and cook until the onion has softened, about 2 minutes. Add the beans, chiles, cumin, and more salt and black pepper and cook until warmed through, 3 to 4 minutes. Mash the beans slightly with a fork. If they seem dry, add a tablespoon or two of water.

Brush a 13 × 9-inch baking dish with a little oil. Spread 2 to 3 tablespoons of the bean filling down the middle of a tortilla, then sprinkle a little shredded cheddar on top. Roll the tortilla around the filling and place it, seam-side down, in the prepared baking dish. Repeat with the remaining tortillas, beans, and cheese. (You want to use about half the cheese here.)

Smother the rolled tortillas with the enchilada sauce, using the back of a spoon to make sure most of the tortillas are covered with sauce, and top with the remaining cheese and red onion. Bake until the cheese is bubbly and golden, 15 to 20 minutes. Serve with your desired toppings.

Serves 4 to 6

## RED ENCHILADA SAUCE

3 tablespoons neutral oil (such as vegetable or canola)

1 tablespoon all-purpose flour

¼ cup chili powder

2 cups vegetable stock, store-bought or homemade (page 232), plus more as needed

1 (14-ounce) can tomato puree

2 teaspoons dried oregano

2 teaspoons smoked paprika

½ teaspoon cayenne pepper

1 teaspoon ground cumin

Kosher salt to taste

In a medium saucepan, heat the oil over medium heat. Add the flour, stirring with a wooden spoon, until golden, about 1 minute. Add the chili powder and cook until it looks darkened, about 30 seconds. Whisk in the stock, tomato puree, oregano, paprika, cayenne, cumin, and salt and stir to combine. Bring to a boil, reduce the heat to low, and cook until slightly darkened in color, about 15 minutes. Use immediately or refrigerate in a storage container for up to 5 days, or freeze for up to 3 months.

Makes 3 cups

tacos, tortillas & enchiladas

FOR THE
holdout

STUFF A FEW TORTILLAS
WITH COOKED SHREDDED PORK
OR CHICKEN—MARK THEM
WITH SOMETHING ON TOP SO
YOU REMEMBER.

# sandwiches & pies

# CRISPY SMOKY TOFU SANDWICHES

We are big fans of the universally beloved crispy fish or chicken sandwiches. We make them all the time—not only on a regular Tuesday night dinner when time is tight but also on a weekend when people are coming over and we can upgrade them by topping with farm-fresh, crunchy slaw and serving alongside crispy potatoes. So in the beginning of Project Plant-Based, I tried a version with tofu, infusing flavor by steeping the tofu "patty" in a soy-saucy marinade and adding dried mustard powder to the panko dredge. It took some time for the kids to come around to it, so for a while there I was frying the tofu and a chicken cutlet in the same pan, creating two decidedly different meals. The front-end prep was exactly the same, though, so it didn't feel like a defeat (or extra work). And eventually, the tofu patty grew on my diners, and the chicken and fish sandwiches disappeared.

2 tablespoons soy sauce

1 tablespoon sambal oelek

3 tablespoons rice vinegar

2 tablespoons neutral oil (such as grapeseed, canola, or vegetable)

1 (14- to 15-ounce) block extra-firm tofu, pressed, drained, and sliced into 4 patty-size pieces, each about 3 × 4 × ½ inches as shown opposite (see page 237; you'll have extra tofu)

1 cup panko bread crumbs

1 tablespoon smoked paprika

2 teaspoons mustard powder

1 teaspoon onion powder

⅛ teaspoon cayenne pepper

Kosher salt and freshly ground black pepper to taste

2 large eggs

¼ cup all-purpose flour

3 tablespoons extra-virgin olive oil, plus more as needed

3 tablespoons mayonnaise

2 teaspoons sriracha sauce

4 potato rolls

2 cups Dill Slaw (page 187)

In a BPA-free zip-top bag, combine the soy sauce, sambal oelek, rice vinegar, oil, and tofu, folding and storing the bag flat in the refrigerator to maximize tofu submersion. Marinate for at least 2 hours and up to 24, flipping the bag every few hours.

When you are ready to eat, set up your dredging stations: In a medium bowl, mix together the panko, paprika, mustard powder, onion powder, cayenne, and some salt and black pepper, then transfer to a large plate. In a shallow bowl, beat the eggs. On a plate, combine the flour with some salt and black pepper.

Heat the olive oil in a deep skillet set over medium-high heat. Remove the tofu pieces from the marinade and gently dry them off with a paper towel. Using your hands, first carefully dredge each tofu piece in the flour mixture, then dip it in the egg (being sure to cover the sides) and coat it thoroughly in the panko (remembering the sides). Add the pieces to the hot oil in the skillet and cook until golden and crispy, about 3 minutes on each side. Once golden, use a spatula to transfer the tofu to a paper-towel-lined plate to drain.

Meanwhile, in a small bowl, mix together the mayo and sriracha.

Sandwich each piece of fried tofu in a roll with some spicy mayo and slaw.

# TOFU BÁNH MÌ

One of the most popular street foods in Vietnam, a bánh mì sandwich is a riot of contrasting textures and flavors—sweet, crunchy pickled carrots and daikon; sriracha-spiked mayo; light-yet-crusty French bread; a little funk from fish sauce, chili peppers, and cilantro; and usually a protein like pâté, pork, or fried tofu. It was always my favorite order at a Vietnamese restaurant, and because there's so much happening in every bite, I just figured I could never replicate it at home. Then I discovered Andrea Nguyen, author of many cookbooks on Vietnamese cooking, including an entire one devoted exclusively to bánh mì. I learned a few crucial rules from her. For starters, you don't want the bread to fight with what's inside, Nguyen says, and to that end, don't use fancy baguettes or buns; you want a roll that possesses a soft interior and is slightly sweet and "commonplace." She also taught me not to overstuff the sandwich with protein. It should resemble a salad in a sandwich. We now make these as regularly as we used to make burgers in our house (especially in the summer), and when it's on the menu, I have dinner on the brain all day long. (I mean that in the best possible way.) It's important to know that in spite of the long list of ingredients, the only real work involved is quick-pickling the vegetables and marinating the tofu, both of which can be done in advance. Once they're made, dinner is strictly an assembly job.

### TOFU

3 tablespoons neutral oil (such as grapeseed, canola, or vegetable)

2 tablespoons mirin

2 tablespoons sambal oelek

2 tablespoons rice vinegar

1 tablespoon soy sauce

1 tablespoon honey

1 (14- to 15-ounce) block extra-firm tofu, pressed, drained, and cut into eight ½-inch-thick pieces as shown opposite (see page 237)

### QUICK-PICKLED VEGETABLES

⅓ cup distilled white vinegar

2 tablespoons sugar

1 teaspoon kosher salt

1 large carrot, shaved into ribbons with a vegetable peeler

1 small daikon radish, or 5 or 6 medium red radishes, peeled and thinly sliced

**PREPARE THE TOFU:** In a BPA-free, zip-top bag, combine the oil, mirin, sambal oelek, rice vinegar, soy sauce, and honey, squishing them to blend thoroughly. Add the tofu and marinate in the refrigerator for at least 3 hours and up to 24.

**MAKE THE QUICK-PICKLED VEGETABLES:** In a small saucepan over medium-high heat, combine the white vinegar, sugar, and salt with 1 cup water. Stir occasionally until the sugar dissolves, about 2 minutes, then add the carrot and radish. Lower the heat and simmer for 5 minutes, then remove the pan from the heat to cool. Let sit until ready to use, or store in a covered container or jar with the cooled liquid for up to 5 days.

CONTINUES

4 small split rolls (like the kind you'd buy for steak sandwiches; you want soft ones), halved lengthwise with some of the interior bread removed

2 tablespoons neutral oil (such as grapeseed, canola, or vegetable)

3 tablespoons mayonnaise

2 teaspoons sriracha sauce

Sliced Persian cucumbers, unpeeled

Fresh cilantro sprigs

6 scallions, white and light green parts only, sliced

Soy sauce, for drizzling

**PREPARE THE SANDWICHES:** When you're ready to make the bánh mì, preheat the oven to 325°F, wrap the rolls in foil, and place them in the oven to warm, 8 to 10 minutes.

Heat the oil in a large nonstick skillet over medium heat. Remove the tofu from the marinade and pan-fry, flipping the pieces gently every 3 minutes until the tofu is golden and crispy around the edges, 6 to 8 minutes total. Transfer the tofu to a paper-towel-lined plate to drain.

Meanwhile, in a small bowl, combine the mayonnaise and sriracha.

To serve, open the rolls, without breaking them, into two pieces. (The two halves should be joined at the hinge.) Spread the spicy mayo on one side of each warmed roll, then add the tofu, quick-pickled vegetables, cucumbers, cilantro, scallions, and a light drizzle of soy sauce. Serve immediately.

**Variation: Bánh Mì–Style Soba Noodles**
*For a dinner that might be considered a close cousin to this tofu bánh mì, skip the bread and the spicy mayo and combine everything else with 8 ounces cooked buckwheat soba noodles. Toss with 1 tablespoon grapeseed oil, 2 teaspoons toasted sesame oil, and 1 teaspoon soy sauce.*

**To vegarize** / OMIT THE HONEY; USE VEGAN OR AVOCADO MAYONNAISE.

**For the holdout** / SWAP OUT THE TOFU FOR A THIN CHICKEN OR PORK CUTLET.

# QUICHE #1: SWEET ONION, SPINACH & CHEDDAR

Is prebaking annoying on a weeknight? Not if you think about it as a stopwatch and your goal is to get everything else assembled in that exact same amount of time. Then it's just "challenging." Spinach-onion-cheddar is an all-time classic combination for quiche, but the truth is, this recipe gives you a basic framework, and you should trust yourself to improvise with whatever vegetables and cheese you add to the egg mixture. My second favorite combination, artichokes and Parm, follows on page 116.

**Store-bought pie dough, such as Pillsbury, to fit a 9-inch pie dish (you might have to roll it slightly)**

**2 tablespoons extra-virgin olive oil**

**1 large white onion, sliced**

**Kosher salt and freshly ground black pepper to taste**

**4 cups loosely packed fresh spinach (or ½ cup thawed, frozen spinach, squeezed dry)**

**½ cup whole milk**

**½ cup half-and-half or light cream**

**4 large eggs**

**3 ounces cheddar cheese, shredded (about ¾ cup)**

Preheat the oven to 375°F. Arrange an oven rack in the middle position.

Fit the dough into a 9-inch pie dish, then using a fork, prick the bottom all over. Bake for 8 minutes.

While the crust parbakes, combine the olive oil, onion, salt, and pepper in a skillet set over medium heat. Cook the onion for as long as you can, stirring occasionally, at least 10 minutes and up to 30 minutes, to get them as caramelized as possible.

Transfer the onion to a cutting board, spreading them out on one side of the board to cool a bit. Add the spinach to the pan and cook, stirring occasionally, until wilted. (Skip this step if using frozen spinach.) Transfer to the same cutting board as the onion and let cool a bit, then roughly chop both the onion and the spinach.

In a medium bowl, whisk together the milk, half-and-half, eggs, and more salt and pepper.

Remove the pie dish from the oven and pour in the egg mixture. Gently add the onion and spinach. Top the whole thing with the cheese and bake until golden on top and a knife inserted into the center comes out clean, 30 to 35 minutes. Let cool about 10 minutes before serving. If you are making this ahead of time, allow it to completely cool, then cover with foil and refrigerate. To reheat, place in the oven, then set the heat to 350°F to warm through (placing the dish in a cold oven allows it to gradually heat with the oven) until a knife inserted into the center comes out hot, about 25 minutes.

Store-bought pie dough, such as Pillsbury, for 1 (9-inch) pie

2 tablespoons extra-virgin olive oil

½ yellow onion, sliced thinly

Shake of dried red pepper flakes

Kosher salt and freshly ground black pepper to taste

1 (14-ounce) can artichoke hearts, drained and finely chopped

½ cup whole milk

½ cup light cream or half-and-half

4 large eggs

⅔ cup grated Parmesan cheese (about 1 ounce)

3 ounces fresh mozzarella, sliced

Preheat the oven to 375°F. Arrange an oven rack in the middle position.

Fit the pie dough into a 9-inch pie dish, then using a fork, prick the bottom all over. Bake for 8 minutes.

While the crust parbakes, combine the olive oil, onion, red pepper flakes, salt, and black pepper in a medium skillet set over medium heat. Cook, stirring occasionally, until the onion is wilted, about 5 minutes. Stir in the artichokes and cook another minute.

Meanwhile, in a medium bowl, whisk together the milk, cream, eggs, Parmesan, and more salt and black pepper.

Remove the pie dish from the oven and immediately pour in the egg mixture. Gently place the onion-artichoke mixture in the filling, distributing it evenly. Arrange the mozzarella slices on top and bake until golden on top and a knife inserted into the center comes out clean, 30 to 35 minutes. Let cool about 10 minutes before serving. If you are making this ahead of time, allow it to completely cool, then cover with foil and refrigerate. To reheat, place in the oven, then set the heat to 350°F to warm through (placing the dish in a cold oven allows it to gradually heat with the oven) until a knife inserted into the center comes out hot, about 25 minutes.

# A COMPETITIVE BURGER

Like a lot of people, we really got into the plant-based burger craze when all the new, impossibly-meaty-tasting patties started showing up in the refrigerated section of our supermarket. We each had our favorites and served them like California-style burgers, piling on the onions and lettuce and homemade "special sauce," remarking over and over, mouths full, "This really *is* almost as good as a hamburger!" But after a while, I started to feel like it maybe wasn't such a great idea to get too addicted to them, especially since the brand we picked up most frequently was highly processed and had an ingredient list as long as a Hostess Twinkie. So I set to work trying to develop a veggie burger with whole ingredients that might take its place.

This was not easy or fun—in fact, if you ever meet my daughters, you might not want to mention the bean-burger phase of testing to either of them. (Though maybe they've blocked it out?) Eventually, I landed on this recipe, which tastes more like a burger and less like a bean. It was originally inspired by a recipe from Sprouted Kitchen's Sara Forte, one of my great heroes of plant-based family cooking. Like many veggie-burger recipes, hers relies on the depth of cooked-down mushrooms and is based on black beans, which I've tried and loved, but I knew the diners at my table—the little ones, at least—would more likely respond to a milder pinto-based burger that also resembled the *color* of a burger. I was right.

And they weren't the only ones who responded favorably. Christine Han, the lovely and talented photographer who shot every picture in this book, told me she couldn't stop thinking about the burgers after eating them at our photo shoot. (When we wrapped, I gave her four frozen patties as a thank-you gift.)

There is a hitch, though. I promised you *easy* vegetarian dinners, and I'm not going to lie, this one is decidedly fussy. *But!* I am so addicted to these burgers that I couldn't *not* include the recipe. Especially since I wound up making a habit of mixing up a batch of patties on Sunday to freeze for my later, less-relaxed weeknight self. If you think ahead to do that, they'll only take 10 minutes to fry up in oil—no thawing required. There you have it, a quick weeknight vegetarian dinner. And so much better than veggie burgers from the supermarket.

CONTINUES

# Veggie Burgers

4 tablespoons extra-virgin
olive oil

½ small yellow onion,
roughly chopped

8 ounces mushrooms
(I use baby bellas), including
stems, chopped

1 cup cooked long- or short-grain
brown rice (I often use Trader Joe's
precooked rice to save myself time)

½ cup old-fashioned rolled oats

½ cup roughly chopped
fresh cilantro

1 large egg

2 tablespoons soy sauce

½ teaspoon garlic powder

½ teaspoon smoked paprika

Kosher salt and freshly ground
black pepper to taste

1 small Japanese sweet potato
(about 7 ounces) or baking potato,
cooked, cooled, flesh scooped out,
and broken into rough chunks

1½ cups cooked pinto beans, or
1 (15-ounce) can, rinsed and drained

¼ cup all-purpose flour,
for dredging

*SERVING*

8 potato buns or brioche buns
(for next-level burgers)

Spicy mayo (3 tablespoons mayo mixed
with 2 teaspoons sriracha; optional)

Pickled Onions (page 231), regular bread-
and-butter pickles, or minced red onions

Crunchy lettuce (optional)

Avocado slices

Pour 2 tablespoons of the olive oil into a cast-iron skillet set over medium heat. After a minute, add the onion and mushrooms and cook, stirring occasionally, until the mushrooms are crispy, 10 to 15 minutes. As the mushrooms cook, they will release a lot of water—you want all the liquid to evaporate from the pan. Set aside to let the mixture cool.

Meanwhile, in a food processor, pulse the brown rice, oats, cilantro, egg, soy sauce, garlic powder, paprika, salt, and pepper until thoroughly combined, about ten 1-second pulses. (Don't overprocess; you want the mixture to be textured—no more than eight to ten pulses.) Add the cooked sweet potato, beans, and cooled mushroom mixture. Pulse until blended but still textured, not even 10 seconds total.

Shape the mixture into 8 very thin 4-inch patties—think California-style. They will probably look mushy and unappetizing, and I implore you not to let any of your diners watch this part, but press on!

(Also, just like with regular burgers, it's easier to shape them when your hands are slightly wet.) After shaping, place the patties on a plate, covered with plastic wrap, and chill in the fridge for about 30 minutes if you have the time. (I've made them without chilling and they're fine, just a little harder to handle in terms of flipping.) If you want to freeze them for a later date, wrap each in parchment paper and place them in a single layer in a resealable freezer bag, set the bag on a plate or cutting board (to stay flat), and freeze for up to 3 months. (You can remove the plate after a few hours.)

When you're ready to eat, heat the remaining 2 tablespoons olive oil in a large skillet, preferably cast iron or nonstick, over medium-high heat. Dredge each patty in flour, then fry until golden and crispy on each side, about 8 minutes total. Serve on buns with your choice of toppings.

Makes 8 burgers

sandwiches & pies

# MUSHROOM-LEEK GALETTE

Every time I make this, Andy says the same thing: "I'd pay $25 for this at a restaurant." He knows that complimenting the cook is 100 percent mandatory in our house, so the praise is not all that unusual, but this particular feedback makes me laugh because it's a dinner I almost always make with store-bought pie dough, frozen peas, and supermarket mushrooms. And look how elegant it is! Would it be better if I used farmers' market hen-of-the-woods mushrooms or wrapped everything up in a homemade pâte brisée? I mean, yeah, of course, but I get a ridiculous amount of pleasure seeing how everyday ingredients can be transformed into something so beautiful and delicious. The other fun thing here? Pressing nutritional yeast right into the dough, which cuts the meatiness a bit with a bright umami surprise. Note this recipe serves 2 for dinner or 4 as a side.

4 tablespoons extra-virgin olive oil

1 large or 2 medium leeks, white parts only, finely chopped (about 3 cups)

Kosher salt and freshly ground black pepper to taste

½ teaspoon dried red pepper flakes

1 pound mushrooms (any kind: cremini, white, shiitake, etc.), stemmed, cleaned, and roughly chopped (about 7 cups)

Leaves from 3 fresh thyme sprigs

⅓ cup frozen peas

1 (9-inch) round of pie dough (store-bought is fine!)

1 tablespoon nutritional yeast

1 large egg, whisked

Flaky sea salt, for sprinkling, preferably Maldon

Preheat the oven to 425°F. Line a sheet pan with parchment paper.

In a large skillet set over medium heat, combine 3 tablespoons of the olive oil, the leeks, salt, black pepper, and red pepper flakes. Cook, stirring occasionally, until the leeks are soft, about 4 minutes. Push the leeks to the perimeter of the pan, then add the remaining 1 tablespoon olive oil and the mushrooms. Cook until the mushrooms have given off their juices and then shriveled, about 10 minutes, leaving the leeks on the perimeter. Stir in the thyme and peas and cook another minute, folding in the leeks.

Place the pie dough on the prepared sheet pan and sprinkle the nutritional yeast all over it, pressing the flakes into the dough with your fingers or a rolling pin. Spoon the mushroom-leek filling into the center, spreading it in an even layer and leaving a 1-inch border, then fold the edges in over the filling, overlapping as you work your way around the perimeter. Brush the dough with the whisked egg and sprinkle with the sea salt. Bake until the crust is golden, 20 to 25 minutes.

*sandwiches & pies*

NUTRITIONAL YEAST
=
BRIGHT UMAMI SURPRISE

# skillet mains

# SPICY CAULIFLOWER FRITTERS *with* PEA SHOOTS

I started experimenting with this meal once I realized that riced cauliflower was now available practically everywhere—from main street groceries to specialty markets. You can think of them as pakora-inspired fritters; they are particularly appealing when served with a mess of bright spring pea shoots (or arugula, watercress, or sprouts) on top.

½ small yellow onion, finely chopped

7 tablespoons extra-virgin olive oil, plus more as needed for frying

1 tablespoon curry powder

¼ teaspoon cayenne pepper

Kosher salt and freshly ground black pepper to taste

12 ounces riced cauliflower (about 6½ cups)

2 large eggs, whisked

⅓ cup panko bread crumbs

¼ cup all-purpose flour

2 tablespoons snipped fresh chives

½ cup frozen peas, thawed

3 ounces pea shoots, arugula, watercress, or sprouts of your choice (about 4 cups)

2 tablespoons fresh lemon juice (from ½ medium lemon)

### SERVING

Plain Greek yogurt

Tamarind sauce, preferably Maggi

In a large nonstick skillet set over medium heat, cook the onion in 3 tablespoons of the olive oil with the curry, cayenne, salt, and black pepper. Cook until wilted, about 2 minutes, stirring often, then add the cauliflower. Continue to cook until everything has softened, about 3 minutes more. Scrape the mixture into a large bowl and let cool for 5 minutes, then mix in the eggs, panko, flour, chives, peas, and more salt and pepper.

Add another 3 tablespoons of the olive oil to the skillet and set over medium-high heat. Spoon a drop of batter into the skillet to make sure the oil is hot enough—you want it to sizzle—then fry ¼-cup scoops of the cauliflower mixture in the oil, flattening each to make fritters. Fry until golden and cooked, about 2 minutes on each side. Transfer the fritters to a large paper-towel-lined platter and tent with foil to keep warm. Repeat with the remaining mixture, adding more oil for frying as needed.

When all the fritters have been cooked, toss the pea shoots with the lemon juice and the remaining 1 tablespoon olive oil in a bowl, then place them on top of the fritters. Serve with plain yogurt and tamarind sauce on the side.

129

*skillet mains*

CRISPY CABBAGE
PANCAKES
132

# CRISPY CABBAGE PANCAKES

This recipe is a quick, decidedly nonauthentic take on okonomiyaki, the iconic Japanese savory pancakes traditionally made with eggs, flour, vegetables, and shrimp or pork. I was originally drawn to the idea of okonomiyaki (which means "what you like, grilled") because it was exactly the kind of dinner I craved on a busy weeknight: something fast, hearty, and fun that worked magic with the odds and ends of whatever I had in the fridge. I also liked that it's an egg-based recipe that isn't an omelet. Riff on this recipe with your favorite vegetable combinations, like shredded carrots or spinach (or even shrimp or pork, if you need to make someone temporarily happy). Just decrease the cabbage accordingly.

3 tablespoons mayonnaise

2 teaspoons sriracha sauce

1 tablespoon plus 1 teaspoon soy sauce

4 large eggs

½ teaspoon kosher salt

½ cup all-purpose flour

5 cups finely shredded cabbage, preferably napa

3 tablespoons finely chopped fresh chives, plus more (optional) for serving

1 bunch scallions, white and light green parts only, finely chopped (about ⅔ cup)

2 tablespoons vegetable oil, plus more as needed

In a small bowl, whisk together the mayo, sriracha, and 1 teaspoon of the soy sauce. Set aside.

In a large bowl, whisk together the eggs, salt, the remaining 1 tablespoon soy sauce, and ⅓ cup water. Gradually whisk in the flour—it's OK if the batter is a little lumpy. Gently fold in the cabbage, chives, and scallions.

Heat the vegetable oil in a large nonstick skillet set over medium heat. Heap ⅓-cup scoops of batter onto the hot surface, using the bottom of the measuring cup or a spoon to gently flatten them. Fry about three at a time, or as many as fit while giving them space. Cook until golden and crispy on each side, 6 to 8 minutes total. Transfer to a plate tented with foil to keep warm. Repeat with the remaining batter, adding more oil to the skillet if necessary. Serve alongside the sriracha dipping sauce and more chives, if desired.

FOR THE holdout / ADD COOKED SHRIMP TO SELECT PATTIES WHERE NECESSARY.

# TOFU with BROCCOLI & SPICY PEANUT SAUCE

The peanut sauce used here (and thinned out with vinegar) is the ultimate hook—so good it's drinkable. If you are contending with tofu resisters (or you are one yourself), this recipe—sweet and spicy, nutty and salty—is a good place to start.

1 tablespoon soy sauce

1 tablespoon sriracha sauce

1 (14- to 15-ounce) block extra-firm tofu, pressed, drained, and sliced into 16 batons (see page 237)

4 tablespoons neutral oil (such as vegetable or grapeseed, or olive oil in a pinch)

2 large bunches broccoli (about 2 pounds), trimmed and roughly chopped

½ small onion, chopped

Kosher salt and freshly ground black pepper to taste

½ cup Spicy Peanut Sauce (page 203)

2 teaspoons rice vinegar

1 bunch scallions, white and light green parts only, minced (about ⅔ cup)

4 lime wedges

Toasted sesame seeds (optional)

Set a large skillet over medium-high heat and add the soy sauce, sriracha, and 1 tablespoon water, stirring to combine. Add the tofu to the pan and, using a spatula or a small spoon, gently flip the batons a few times, to cover them with the glaze. Let sit for 2 minutes and wait for everything to start sizzling a little. Using a spatula, gently flip the tofu batons and cook for another 2 minutes, drizzling in 1 tablespoon of the oil to prevent sticking. When they are deep orange and look lacquered, about 2 minutes more, remove them from the skillet to a wire rack and add the remaining 3 tablespoons oil to the skillet.

Add the broccoli, onion, salt, and pepper to the skillet and stir only occasionally, allowing the broccoli to get crispy and brown in patches, 10 to 12 minutes. Using a slotted spoon, evenly distribute the broccoli among four shallow dinner bowls. Place the tofu batons on top of the broccoli.

In a small measuring cup or bowl, whisk the peanut sauce with the rice vinegar until it reaches a dressing-like consistency. Drizzle a little on top of each bowl, along with scallions, a squeeze of lime, and sesame seeds, if using. Alternatively, place all the toppings in small bowls on the table and let diners garnish their bowls themselves.

/ vegan /

# TERIYAKI-GLAZED CRISPY TOFU
## with GREEN BEANS

If the story of tofu acceptance at my family's dinner table were a movie, the climactic scene—run in slow motion and set to orchestral music—would be the night I made this recipe. More specifically, it would be the moment Abby picked a golden-glazed cube out of the pan and said to me, "Are you sure that's enough for all four of us?" (Translation: *I like this very much, and I need to make sure I eat a lot of it in the immediate future.*) I tried to play it cool and assured her we'd be just fine. Then I proceeded to watch her eat everything on her plate. Who knows if it was the Teriyaki speaking (as I've mentioned, the sauce has a powerful hold on my family), but it's more likely because the tofu is dredged in cornstarch before being fried and glazed, resulting in a universally crowd-pleasing crisp-tender tofu cube. Serve this right away so the tofu retains its crispiness, either alone or with white rice. Also, I like the French beans because they are skinnier (thus quick-cooking) and usually more flavorful.

1 (14- to 15-ounce) container extra-firm tofu, pressed, drained, and cut into 1-inch cubes (see page 237)

3 tablespoons cornstarch

1 teaspoon onion powder

¼ cup neutral oil (such as grapeseed, vegetable, or canola), plus more as needed

12 ounces fresh green beans, preferably French (haricots verts), or thawed frozen, if fresh beans aren't in season

1 (1-inch) piece fresh ginger, peeled and minced (about 1 tablespoon)

1 bunch scallions, white and light green parts only, roughly chopped (about ⅔ cup)

1 garlic clove, halved

⅓ cup Teriyaki Sauce (page 211)

In a large bowl, gently toss the tofu in the cornstarch and onion powder until the cubes are lightly coated.

Heat the oil in a large deep skillet set over medium-high heat until the oil is hot and looks shiny. Add the tofu cubes to the pan carefully, making sure they aren't crowded together. (If there's not enough space, it's a good idea to fry them in batches.) Fry, stirring only occasionally to allow for browning, until crispy on all sides, about 5 minutes total. Using a slotted spoon, transfer the tofu to a paper-towel-lined plate.

Reduce the heat to medium, adding a little more oil as needed, and add the beans. Cook and toss until cooked through. If your beans are fresh and raw, this might take up to 10 minutes; if you use thawed frozen, it will take more like 5. Add the ginger, scallions, and garlic, stirring with the beans until the aromatics smell fragrant, another 2 minutes. Drizzle in the teriyaki sauce and toss until everything is coated. Gently toss in the tofu, adding a little more sauce if necessary (be judicious, though—it's sweet!) and serve right away.

/ vegan /

# MUSHROOM–BOK CHOY PACKED FRIED RICE

Fried rice is another one of those recipes that can transform a little bit of this and a little bit of that into a lotta something special. And you know how it used to be the kind of dish you'd only think to make when you had day-old rice? Thanks to the precooked rice you can find in most supermarket freezer aisles these days, you can now make it whenever the spirit moves you. (I just let the frozen rice thaw on the counter for a half hour.) The important thing to know going in is that this recipe requires patience—something I do not have in spades—which means allowing each component (the aromatics, the rice, the vegetables, the eggs) to brown and crisp in their own time. My secret is using porcini powder, which you can find online and usually in better supermarkets, because it lends the dish a meatiness that someone might miss with the omission of chicken or pork. (Mushroom powder in general is also a good thing to have in your vegetarian box of tricks if you love the deep flavor of mushrooms but are cooking for people who don't necessarily like the *sight* of mushrooms.) Lastly, let yourself think of this recipe as a general template for fried rice—I love bok choy, but spinach, peas, kale, and cooked broccoli can all stand in or lend support. The goal here is to pack the rice full of vegetables.

**6 tablespoons neutral oil (such as vegetable or canola), plus more as needed**

**1 tablespoon toasted sesame oil**

**1 (1-inch) piece fresh ginger, peeled and minced**

**½ medium red onion, chopped into 1-inch chunks**

**Shake of dried red pepper flakes**

**2 teaspoons mushroom powder (I like porcini)**

**8 ounces thinly sliced mushrooms (any kind; I use baby bella, white, or shiitake)**

**3 to 4 baby bok choy stalks (14 to 16 ounces), roughly chopped (including stems)**

**4 cups room-temperature cooked brown rice (preferably day-old) or thawed frozen precooked rice (such as Trader Joe's brand)**

**2 large eggs, whisked**

**1 tablespoon rice wine vinegar**

**3 tablespoons soy sauce**

Add 2 tablespoons of the vegetable oil and all the sesame oil to a wok or large nonstick skillet set over medium heat.

Add the ginger, onion, and red pepper flakes, and cook until the onion has softened, about 2 minutes. Add the mushroom powder and cook another minute until it darkens and smells toasty. Push the aromatics to the perimeter of the pan and add another tablespoon of oil to the center. Add the mushrooms, and cook until they've released most of their liquid, about 8 minutes. Add the bok choy and cook until wilted, 2 minutes more, mixing in the aromatics at the end. Using a slotted spoon, remove the vegetables from the pan to a bowl.

Increase the heat to medium-high and add the remaining vegetable oil. Add the rice and use a spatula to flatten it into one layer as much as possible, so every grain is crisping up on the pan's hot surface. Cook without stirring for 3 to 4 minutes, to allow for crisping. Toss and flip a little, then cook another 2 minutes without stirring, to get the other grains crispy.

**Sriracha or hot sauce**

Move the rice to the perimeter of the pan and decrease the heat to medium-low. Add the eggs to the center, and stir only occasionally to allow large chunks to form. Gradually stir the rice into the eggs, then add the reserved vegetables to the pan, cooking everything until the eggs have reached desired doneness (we like ours tender, very slightly wet), about 1 minute more. Drizzle in the rice wine vinegar and soy sauce and toss. Serve in bowls with sriracha or hot sauce.

# SPICY CHICKPEAS with TOMATOES & GREENS

This meal is a revelation because it's healthy, crazy flavorful . . . and made almost entirely from canned pantry staples that you probably always have on hand. (We call this "can-to-table" cooking in our house—you heard it here first!) It typically shows up on our family dinner table toward the end of the week, when there's little left from the previous weekend's shop. I added fresh kale in this version (because kale is hardy and is usually still in relatively good shape at the end of the week), but you can just as easily use thawed frozen spinach or peas if that's what's in your freezer.

2 tablespoons grapeseed or vegetable oil

½ small yellow onion, finely chopped

1 medium garlic clove, minced

1 (1-inch) piece fresh ginger, peeled and minced

Dried red pepper flakes to taste

Kosher salt and freshly ground black pepper to taste

3 tablespoons curry powder

1 tablespoon tomato paste

3 cups cooked chickpeas, or 2 (15-ounce) cans, rinsed, drained, and dried as much as possible

1 (14.5-ounce) can diced tomatoes

½ to 1 cup vegetable stock, store-bought or homemade (page 232)

2 cups stemmed and chopped fresh kale, or ½ cup thawed frozen kale, squeezed dry

1 teaspoon white miso

¼ cup light coconut milk

### SERVING

Steamed rice or store-bought naan, or Yogurt Flatbread (page 222)

Lime wedges

Chopped fresh cilantro

In a large skillet set over medium-low heat, combine the oil, onion, garlic, ginger, red pepper flakes, salt, and black pepper and cook until slightly softened, 4 to 5 minutes. Increase the heat to medium, stir in the curry powder, and cook to allow it to toast a bit, 4 or 5 minutes. Add the tomato paste, smushing it into the onion with a wooden spoon. Cook another minute until the red color darkens and it smells toasty. Add the chickpeas and stir to coat them with the curry mixture. Cook until they look like they are slightly crispy, about 5 minutes. Taste a chickpea and, if you think the dish needs more seasoning, adjust accordingly.

Stir in the tomatoes and ½ cup of the stock and simmer on the stovetop for another 10 minutes or so, until everything is warmed through. (If it looks too thick, add up to the remaining ½ cup vegetable broth to loosen it.) Add the kale and cook until wilted.

Stir the miso into ¼ cup warm water and add it to the skillet along with the coconut milk. Cook about 2 minutes more, until warmed through, then serve with rice or bread, a lime wedge, and a sprinkle of cilantro.

/ vegan /

# CRISPY CHICKPEAS with NAAN & YOGURT SAUCE

A version of this recipe appeared in my last book, *How to Celebrate Everything*, but I make it so frequently, it felt wrong not to include it in the book devoted to my go-to weeknight vegetarian dinners. It's the kind of homey comfort-food meal I make when I'm cooking for myself, and I enjoy it the most when eaten standing up, leaning against the counter, and reading the news. It's so ridiculously simple, I worry that calling it "cooking" is overstating things. Yes, you fry the chickpeas, but that's as hard as it gets. The key is to make sure you have the right things to dollop and drizzle on top: a good tamarind sauce (*Indian-ish* cookbook author Priya Krishna changed my life when she steered me in the direction of Maggi brand) and a yogurt with at least 2% fat content.

**3 cups Crispy Chickpeas (page 198)**

**¾ cup plain yogurt (whole-milk or 2%)**

**Tamarind sauce, preferably Maggi, to taste**

**½ cup chopped fresh cilantro, leaves and stems**

### SERVING

**4 store-bought naans or pitas, or 4 Yogurt Flatbreads (page 222), toasted**

Divide the chickpeas among the plates and top each with a dollop of yogurt, a generous drizzling of tamarind sauce, and cilantro and serve with naan.

# CRUNCHY-CHEESY BEAN BAKE

There are two things going on with this 30-minute dinner that will probably appeal to kids: (1) the crunchy and (2) the cheesy. I love how those melty mozzarella rounds recall a classic baked chicken Parm—but there's not an obscene amount of cheese. The recipe as written makes enough for four medium portions. Pair it with a simple green salad (or Our Favorite Kale Salad with Almonds & Dried Cranberries, page 174) and some crusty bread.

6 tablespoons extra-virgin olive oil

½ medium yellow onion, finely chopped

2 garlic cloves, minced

Pinch of dried red pepper flakes

Kosher salt and freshly ground black pepper to taste

1 heaping tablespoon tomato paste

1 (14.5-ounce) can diced tomatoes

1 tablespoon dried oregano

3 cups cooked white beans, such as gigantes or cannellini, or 2 (15-ounce) cans, rinsed and drained

1 cup panko bread crumbs

¼ cup grated Parmesan cheese

Leaves from 3 fresh thyme sprigs

5 thin slices fresh mozzarella (about 3 ounces)

Preheat the oven to 400°F.

Heat 3 tablespoons of the olive oil in a deep, large oven-safe skillet over medium heat. Stir in the onion, garlic, red pepper flakes, salt, and black pepper and cook until the onion is soft, about 3 minutes.

Add the tomato paste and smush it in with a wooden spoon until the onion becomes pink and the paste gets toasty and deepens in color a bit. Stir in the tomatoes, oregano, and ¼ cup water, increase the heat to medium-high, and cook until warmed through, about another 5 minutes. Add the beans and cook, stirring occasionally, until they are warmed through, another 4 to 5 minutes.

While the beans warm, prepare your panko topping. In a small bowl, use a fork to mix together the panko, Parm, thyme, and the remaining 3 tablespoons olive oil until every crumb is glistening.

Arrange the mozzarella slices over the warm beans, then, using your hands, evenly sprinkle the panko around the slices, covering as much of the beans as possible. Transfer the skillet to the oven and bake for 15 minutes, until bubbly and golden. Sometimes I broil this at the very end to help along the browning.

# CAULIFLOWER CUTLETS with ROMESCO SAUCE

I still get nervous if the kids ask me, "What's for dinner?" when I'm making something like this, something that is hard to get their heads around before trying it. Cauliflower steak? What even is that? I can barely get them to eat my favorite impossible-to-hate cauliflower dish—roasted with anchovy bread crumbs. But this time, I saved the debut of this dinner for a night when they were starving. It worked. Abby likened the final product to her favorite Lowcountry specialty: fried green tomatoes. Phoebe was so hungry I don't know if she noticed that she was eating fried cauliflower as opposed to chicken. Note #1: If florets break off the main stalk, save them and do a quick sauté with scallions or onions after the cutlets are fried and done. Note #2: We've also made this swapping out the romesco for Herby Buttermilk Ranch (page 216) with wonderful results. Note #3: If you have leftover romesco, it is delicious spread on a baguette slice or with raw vegetables.

½ cup all-purpose flour

2 eggs, whisked

1 cup panko bread crumbs

Kosher salt and freshly ground black pepper to taste

2 tablespoons nutritional yeast

3 tablespoons extra-virgin olive oil, plus more as needed

1 large head cauliflower (about 2½ pounds), outer leaves removed, sliced from top to bottom into 6 to 8 (¾-inch) "steaks"

Chopped fresh chives

### ROMESCO SAUCE

1 (12-ounce) jar roasted sweet red peppers, completely drained

1 garlic clove

2 teaspoons red wine vinegar

Kosher salt and freshly ground black pepper to taste

½ cup blanched sliced almonds

⅓ cup extra-virgin olive oil

First set up the dredging stations in three wide bowls: one for the flour, one for the eggs, and one for the panko mixed with the salt, pepper, and nutritional yeast.

Heat the olive oil in a large skillet over medium-high heat. Using your fingers, dredge a cauliflower steak first with flour, then dip it in egg, and finally coat it in the seasoned panko. Place it in the hot skillet, and repeat with as many remaining steaks as will fit in the pan without overcrowding. (You'll have to do the frying in batches.) Fry each steak until golden and crispy, about 6 minutes total, flipping gently with a wide metal spatula about halfway through. Transfer the steaks to a paper-towel-lined plate to drain. If a few pieces of the coating fall off, scoop them out onto the paper towel, too. Repeat until all the cauliflower has been breaded and fried.

**MEANWHILE, MAKE THE ROMESCO SAUCE:** In a blender or small food processor, combine the roasted peppers, garlic, vinegar, salt, black pepper, almonds, and olive oil and blend until emulsified. You want the sauce to be spreadable, so it should be on the thicker side.

To serve, spread ½ cup romesco sauce on each dinner plate. Place one or two cauliflower steaks in the middle and top with chives.

FOR THE
holdout / BREAD AND FRY A REGULAR CHICKEN CUTLET IF THAT'S WHAT IT TAKES.

# small plates night

A LIBERATING WAY TO THINK ABOUT ASSEMBLING VEGETARIAN DINNERS

ROASTED
EGGPLANT &
TOMATOES WITH
MISO-TAHINI
SAUCE (PAGE 178)

**IN ALL MY YEARS** writing about feeding picky kids, one of the most popular strategies I ever came up with was called Muffin Tin Tapas, in which I suggested filling each cup of a muffin tin with something different. It was easy to assemble and had built-in No-Touching Protection™, and, best of all, kids seemed to enjoy things more when they had a lot of little tastes, as opposed to only three big things piled high on something so boring as a plate. "The magic is in the mix," I wrote, and I might as well have been talking about tapas or meze or dim sum, or any of the many cuisines around the world that have a tradition of small-plate dining. Once my family decided to lean more vegetarian and I was no longer beholden to the protein-starch-veg dinner formula I grew up with, the small-plates strategy became a very appealing way to think about cooking—for everyone at the table, not just the bullheaded kids. A little of this, a little of that. Some stuff homemade, some store-bought. A plate of warm, fresh bread, plus a bowl of something legumey (lentils, brothy beans, hummus) surrounded by one or two vegetable-driven dishes? Man, I could eat like that every night—especially when the weather gets warm and you barely have to do anything to make the small plates of vegetables taste extraordinary. (I call those "The Vegetable Is the Star" salads.) This section is devoted to that kind of eating and follows a more liberating kind of formula: Pick one bean dish, one bread dish, and a few of the vegetable sides. Muffin tins optional.

# HOW TO ASSEMBLE A SMALL-PLATES DINNER

**START WITH**
**BEANS**

Herby, Brothy Lima Beans 160

Coconut Curried Red Lentils 162

Marinated Beans 163

The Creamiest Hummus 164

**+**

**THEN**
**BREAD**

Za'atar Pizza Dough Flatbread 220

Yogurt Flatbread 222

Honey-Crusted Skillet Corn Bread 224

Warmed baguette or crusty boule (store-bought)

**+**

**ADD**
**VEGETABLES**

Peppery Sprout Salad with Avocado 170

Shredded Carrot Salad with Yogurt-Harissa Sauce 170

Roasted Beets with Quick-Pickled Cabbage & Dill 171

Hot Honey Brussels Sprouts 172

Steamed Kale with Spicy Peanut Sauce 172

Chopped Broccolini Salad with Dill & Feta 173

Any-Which-Way Chopped, Charred Broccolini 173

Our Favorite Kale Salad with Almonds & Dried Cranberries 174

Slivered Minty Sugar Snap Peas on a Bed of Ricotta 174

Roasted Beets with Herby Yogurt & Pistachios 176

Roasted Eggplant & Tomatoes with Miso-Tahini Sauce 178

Greek-Style Lemon-Oregano Potatoes 180

Andy's Spicy Diced Potatoes 182

Brown Butter Corn with Parsley 184

Sesame Bok Choy 184

Tomato Salad with Avocado-Basil Dressing 186

Tomato-Nectarine Salad 186

Dill Slaw 187

Coconutty Avocado Toasts 187

Roasted Honeynut Squash with Crispy Sage Leaves 188

Restuffed Japanese Sweet Potatoes with Miso & Chives 190

**=**

**DINNER**

**2**

**3**

**4**

*SUGGESTED COMBO N° 1*

**1** Yogurt
Flatbread 222
+
**2** Shredded
Carrot Salad with
Yogurt-Harissa
Sauce 170
+
**3** Hot Honey
Brussels Sprouts
172
+
**4** Roasted Beets
with Quick-
Pickled Cabbage
& Dill 171
+
**5** The Creamiest
Hummus 164

**3**

**1**

4

5

2

SUGGESTED
COMBO Nº 3

1 Crusty Bread
+
2 Marinated
Beans 163
+
3 Coconutty
Avocado Toasts
187
+
4 Our Favorite
Kale Salad with
Almonds & Dried
Cranberries
174
+
BONUS
BURRATA!

bonus:
BURRATA!

1

3

4

3

4

3

2

# Herby, Brothy Lima Beans

I'm not providing alternative instructions for using canned beans here, because the beans' simmering broth (and the beans themselves if you are lucky enough to start with heirloom limas) is what makes this simple dish so flavorful and special. (Truly, you might never go back to canned.) If you only have canned beans at your disposal, I suggest using the marinade recipe on page 163. This can also be done in an Instant Pot or pressure cooker; just skip the presoaking and cook using the high pressure setting for 25 minutes.

**16 ounces dried lima beans**

**½ medium yellow onion, roughly chopped**

**1 tablespoon kosher salt**

**¼ cup extra-virgin olive oil, plus more for drizzling**

**1 dried bay leaf**

**Leaves from 8 fresh thyme sprigs**

**1 tablespoon fresh lemon juice**

**Store-bought pesto, for serving (optional)**

**Freshly grated Parmesan, for serving (optional; omit for vegans)**

Place the lima beans in a large pot, cover with water by about 2 inches, and let them sit for at least 6 hours and up to overnight, 8 to 10 hours. Check them periodically and add water to keep them slightly submerged.

Add more water to cover the beans by 1½ inches and place on the stovetop. Stir in the onion, salt, olive oil, and bay leaf. Simmer uncovered, until tender, about 40 minutes, scraping off any foam as they cook.

Once tender, do not drain the beans. Scoop them into a small serving bowl with a little of the bean broth. Finish with a drizzle of olive oil, a few thyme leaves, some lemon juice, and pesto and Parmesan, if using.

Makes 4 cups

 / vegan /

small plates night

## Coconut Curried Red Lentils

It's shocking how fast this dish comes together, especially given how flavorful it is. I often make it for a warm lunch on a cold winter day.

2 tablespoons coconut oil

½ small yellow onion, finely chopped

1 (1-inch) piece fresh ginger, peeled and finely minced (about 1 tablespoon)

1 garlic clove, minced

Kosher salt and freshly ground black pepper to taste

1 tablespoon hot curry powder

2 cups dried red lentils (about 14 ounces)

1 tablespoon white miso

4 cups vegetable stock, store-bought or homemade (page 232)

*SERVING*

Plain yogurt (optional; omit to keep vegan)

Chopped fresh cilantro

Lime wedges

3 or 4 scallions, light green and white parts only, minced

*small plates night*

In a medium soup pot, melt the coconut oil over medium-low heat. Add the onion, ginger, garlic, salt, and pepper and cook until the vegetables have softened, about 2 minutes. Stir in the curry powder and cook until aromatic and toasty, another minute. Add the lentils, stirring until they are coated with oil.

In a small bowl or measuring cup, mix the miso with ¼ cup water. Add the vegetable stock and miso mix to the soup pot and bring to a boil. Reduce to a simmer, stirring occasionally, and cook until the lentils are just softened and starting to lose their shape, 10 to 12 minutes.

Transfer the lentils to a shallow serving bowl, top with the plain yogurt (if using), cilantro, a squeeze of lime juice, and scallions, and serve.

Serves 4

/ vegan /

# Marinated Beans

Think of this recipe the way you think of marinating meat—the longer those beans sit in this bright, herby blend, the more flavorful your dinner becomes. The only hard part is remembering to do it a few hours ahead of time, but even if you have only a half hour, marinating will give your beans a little boost. I find it is an especially effective technique for freshening up canned beans.

¼ cup red wine vinegar

⅓ cup extra-virgin olive oil

1 garlic clove, halved

Kosher salt and freshly ground
black pepper to taste

8 fresh basil leaves, chopped, or
1 rosemary sprig, left whole

Shake of dried red pepper flakes

3 cups cooked beans, such as cranberry,
cannellini, or great northern, or
2 (15-ounce) cans, rinsed and drained

In a medium bowl, whisk together the vinegar, olive oil, garlic, salt, black pepper, basil, and red pepper flakes. Toss in the beans, stir, cover with plastic wrap, and let marinate in the refrigerator for as long as you have—up to overnight, tossing every hour when possible. Keeps in the refrigerator for 3 to 5 days.

Makes 4 small plate portions

/ vegan /

# The Creamiest Hummus

At least a few times a month, I try to hit the legendary Brooklyn Middle Eastern market Sahadi's for their mind-blowing hummus. Smooth, slightly lemony, and creamy-to-the-point-of-pourable, it is beyond superior to any store-bought version in my neck of the woods, and eventually my family wouldn't accept any other kind. When I tried to re-create it at home during 2020's coronavirus quarantine, my spoiled kids were ruthless in their criticism. Too thick. Too garlicky. Too this, too that, too *it-doesn't-taste-like-Sahadi's*. Finally, I made two members of the family stand next to me and advise while I whirled my cooked-from-scratch Rancho Gordo chickpeas in the food processor. "Creamier," they cried. "Saltier! Why can't I taste the lemon?" Then, finally, "Stop! It's perfect." Like all the recipes in this book that call for beans, your final result will be better if you use dried beans instead of canned, and that is especially true of hummus.

Pulse the chickpeas 8 to 10 times in a food processor until rough and pasty. Add the tahini, garlic, lemon juice, kosher salt, and ice water. Process until smooth, adding more ice water as needed until it reaches your desired consistency. We like it super smooth so I usually end up adding up to another ½ cup water. Serve on a platter drizzled with good olive oil and sprinkled with sea salt and paprika. Store in an airtight container in the refrigerator for up to 1 week.

### VARIATIONS

*For green hummus, add ½ cup packed thawed frozen spinach (squeezed of excess liquid) plus another tablespoon of lemon juice with the remaining ingredients after pulsing the chickpeas; garnish with a few thawed frozen peas, if desired. For pink hummus, whirl in 1 large or 2 small peeled cooked beets with the remaining ingredients after pulsing the chickpeas. Serve with sliced radishes if you have them.*

Makes 3½ cups

/ vegan /

3 cups cooked chickpeas, or 2 (15-ounce) cans, rinsed and drained

½ cup tahini

1 large garlic clove, smashed and roughly chopped

¼ cup fresh lemon juice (from 1 medium lemon)

½ teaspoon kosher salt

½ cup ice-cold water, plus more as needed

*SERVING*

Extra-virgin olive oil, for drizzling

Flaky sea salt, preferably Maldon

Sweet paprika

*small plates night*

# A Note About Beans

Before we became weekday vegetarians, there were essentially two bean-based recipes in our regular family dinner rotation that we could count on our kids eating: black bean burritos (still one of the most popular on my website—look it up!) and baked beans, which I'd prepare as follows: Purchase two cans of Bush's Original Baked Beans (the kind with the hunk of ham in there), dump them into a pot, heat, and serve alongside turkey burgers. Sometimes, like the sophisticates we were—and much to the girls' delight—we'd dump our Bush's beans on toast and turn on some Premier League soccer. But that was pretty much the extent of our bean repertoire when it came to meals the girls could get excited about. I'm really not kidding about this. It's not even that I don't like beans. Andy and I have always *loved* them—Giuliano Bugialli's famous minestrone would be a serious contender for My Last Meal, and both of us get irrationally excited about heirloom varieties we discover in markets and online—but we just couldn't land on the recipes that would entice the girls over to our side.

As any vegetarian could've told us, this was going to have to change if our Eat Less Meat Plan was going to be in any way sustainable. They're too convenient, too versatile, and too protein-rich not to exploit for fast

vegetarian family dinners. From Day 1 of this project, I never left the supermarket without a wildcard bag of lentils or a can or two of chickpeas and black, white, or pinto beans. And every time I experimented with a bean recipe—keeping in mind dishes my family might order in restaurants and combinations that capitalized on their favorite flavors—it felt like I was using an unofficial litmus test: Are they as excited about this as their beloved Bush's?

On the subject of cans: For better or worse, since I imagine you are more than likely referring to this book on days when you feel the need to start dinner before even taking off your coat, every bean recipe I've included assumes you have not thought ahead to overnight-soak and simmer your dried beans. Obviously, your beans will taste better and fresher when you cook them from scratch yourself, but canned beans are perfectly fine to use, too. They are your loyal friends in your transition to more meat-free meals: dependable, flexible, and *always* there when you need them.

Having said that, once you've cooked with good-quality dried beans and tasted how creamy and flavorful they can be with the infusion of aromatics and herbs, it's hard to go back to canned. Before our Weekday

Vegetarian pledge, I'd only really been able to cook with dried beans on the weekend, when I'd thought ahead to soak and simmer and make a big batch of them to last throughout the week. Once they became a mainstay in the dinner rotation, I decided it was finally time to purchase a pressure cooker. A pressure cooker allows you to skip the overnight soaking routine and gives you tender, cooked lovelies within 45 minutes (sometimes less) of announcing you'll be eating beans for dinner. I am not a gadget person— even the ever-popular slow cooker is collecting dust on an upper shelf somewhere—but given how much more we were relying on and planning our meals around heirloom dried beans like corona and cranberry and lima, it did seem like I'd get a good return on investment with an Instant Pot. Even though beans are just about the only thing I use it for, I think it's worth the investment. Add a regular bean delivery from the amazing Rancho Gordo heirloom suppliers in California and ask me if I miss that strip steak.

OK, maybe don't ask me that. But you get the point. The recipes in this book work with whatever bean you think you can handle on any given night, be it dried beans or canned. And I'm pleased to report that our Bush's days are (mostly) behind us.

# BREADS

1

## Peppery
## Sprout Salad
## with Avocado

This benefits significantly from the addition of a Seven-Minute Egg (page 197). Add one egg per salad.

- 5 cups sprouts, such as arugula, pea, or watercress sprouts
- ¼ cup extra-virgin olive oil, plus more for drizzling
- 2 tablespoons fresh lemon juice
- Kosher salt and tons of freshly ground black pepper, to taste
- 2 avocados, peeled, pitted, and cut into quartered wedges
- Vegetarian furikake (optional)

Toss the sprouts in a large bowl with the olive oil, lemon juice, salt, and pepper. Divide among four plates and top each with 2 avocado wedges, furikake (if using), and another drizzle of olive oil.

**Makes 4 small plates**

/ vegan /

## Shredded Carrot
## Salad with
## Yogurt-Harissa Sauce

If you are using the shredding attachment of your food processor, process the onions along with the carrots to make it a little easier on yourself.

- 6 medium carrots, shredded (about 4 cups; store-bought preshredded is fine)
- 2 tablespoons very thinly sliced red onion
- ⅔ cup Yogurt-Harissa Sauce (page 208)
- ¼ cup chopped fresh flat-leaf parsley

In a large bowl, toss the carrots and onion with the yogurt-harissa sauce. Shower with parsley and serve.

**Makes 4 small plates**

# Roasted Beets with Quick-Pickled Cabbage & Dill

In addition to being delicious, this wins the prize for prettiest and pinkest. Look for purple napa cabbages at farm markets whenever possible, and remember that there is no shame in picking up the precooked shrink-wrapped beets in the produce section to help this along faster.

4 to 5 cups cooled, Roasted Beets (recipe follows)

1 to 1½ cups chopped Quick-Pickled Cabbage (recipe follows), or to taste

⅓ cup chopped fresh dill

3 tablespoons extra-virgin olive oil

3 tablespoons finely chopped scallions, light green and white parts only

Kosher salt and freshly ground black pepper to taste

In a salad bowl, toss together the roasted beets, pickled cabbage, dill, olive oil, scallions, salt, and pepper.

Makes 4 small plates

 / vegan /

## ROASTED BEETS

18 to 20 ounces small beets, mixed varieties and colors, as evenly sized as possible, unpeeled

Extra-virgin olive oil

Kosher salt to taste

Preheat the oven to 375°F.

In a large bowl, toss the beets with a generous drizzle of olive oil (just to coat—not to drench the beets) and a sprinkle of salt. Divide the beets and wrap them in two separate foil packets. Roast for 1 hour 30 minutes. Open the packets, letting steam escape, and allow to cool.

Once they are cool, slip the skins off with your fingers, rinse, dry, and quarter each beet.

## QUICK-PICKLED CABBAGE

2 cups loosely packed napa cabbage, separated or chopped into small leaves and wedges

½ cup red wine vinegar

2 tablespoons sugar

1 tablespoon kosher salt

Place the cabbage pieces in a 12-ounce jar. In a small saucepan, simmer 1 cup water with the vinegar, sugar, and salt until the sugar dissolves. Let the pickling liquid cool slightly, then pour it over the cabbage in the jar. Let the cabbage pieces steep for as long as possible. They'll be flavorful after 10 or 15 minutes if you need them right away, but it's ideal to let them sit in their liquid overnight. The cabbage will keep covered in the refrigerator for up to 2 weeks.

## Hot Honey Brussels Sprouts

If you can't find hot honey (I love chili-infused Mike's Hot Honey), just use regular honey and sprinkle about ¼ teaspoon cayenne pepper all over the Brussels sprouts. Also, I encourage you to just eyeball the honey measurement (you know what a tablespoon looks like, I know you do!), because drizzling honey is so much less of a chore than measuring out two sticky teaspoons. I often serve these piled on top of hummus (page 164).

4 cups trimmed and halved Brussels sprouts (about 16 ounces)

½ small onion, chopped

¼ cup extra-virgin olive oil

1 tablespoon hot honey

Kosher salt and freshly ground black pepper to taste

1 tablespoon red wine vinegar

Preheat the oven to 425°F. Line a sheet pan with foil.

Place the Brussels sprouts and onion on the prepared sheet pan. Drizzle the olive oil, honey, salt, and pepper on top and toss with your hands, making sure all the Brussels are coated and shiny. Roast until they are crispy and golden, about 25 minutes. Remove to a bowl and drizzle with the vinegar.

**Makes 4 small plates**

## Steamed Kale with Spicy Peanut Sauce

Here, the traditional spinach is swapped for kale in my favorite Japanese vegetable side dish, goma-ae.

1 pound curly kale, cleaned, stemmed, and chopped into 1-inch pieces

2 tablespoons extra-virgin olive oil

Kosher salt and freshly ground black pepper to taste

4 tablespoons Spicy Peanut Sauce (page 203), thinned a little with warm water to be drizzling consistency

3 tablespoons toasted sesame seeds

Steam the kale in batches until wilted, about 3 minutes, and remove it to a medium bowl. Toss lightly with the olive oil, salt, and pepper. Divide among 4 serving bowls and drizzle each with a tablespoon of the peanut sauce and a sprinkling of sesame seeds.

**Makes 4 small plates**

/ vegan /

small plates night

## Chopped Broccolini Salad with Dill & Feta

In the winter, when the greens are not so hot, I love thinking about Broccolini as a replacement for them in a salad. To get Broccolini salad-ready, you just have to boil, shock, and chop. The resulting texture—a mix of tender leaves and crunchy stems—is way more exciting than any plastic-bagged spring medley. If you can't find Broccolini, you can swap in regular broccoli.

Kosher salt

1½ pounds Broccolini, including thin stems (you can trim and discard thicker stems)

2 tablespoons minced red onion

3 ounces crumbled feta (just about 1 cup)

1 tablespoon chopped fresh dill

3 tablespoons white balsamic vinegar

¼ cup extra-virgin olive oil

Prepare an ice bath by filling a large bowl with ice water.

Bring a large pot of heavily salted water to a boil and add the Broccolini. Cook until the Broccolini is crisp-tender, about 4 minutes, then, using tongs, transfer the Broccolini to the ice water to stop the cooking and preserve its bright green color. Drain in a colander and pat dry with paper towels or a kitchen towel.

Roughly chop the Broccolini, making sure the stems are chopped into small pieces, then transfer this to a salad bowl (it can be the same large bowl you used for the ice bath, dried). Add the onion, feta, dill, vinegar, and olive oil and toss to combine.

**Makes 4 small plates**

## Any-Which-Way Chopped, Charred Broccolini

This is my most favorite way to prepare Broccolini, which sits a little flatter in a skillet than regular broccoli. I love the skillet method because it yields a guaranteed easy sell at the table, and also because it benefits from my laziness—the more hands-off I am, the more charred and crispy it gets.

5 tablespoons extra-virgin olive oil

2 pounds Broccolini, trimmed of rough stems

Kosher salt and freshly ground pepper

¼ cup chopped red onion

*SERVING (OPTIONAL)*
Drizzle of aged balsamic vinegar; or shake of furikake and drizzle of soy sauce and rice wine vinegar; or squeeze of lemon juice and sprinkle of grated Parmesan cheese (omit for vegans)

In a large (this is key!) skillet, heat 4 tablespoons of the olive oil over medium-high heat. Add the Broccolini, salt, and pepper and let it sit without stirring for least 5 minutes, then toss and let it sit undisturbed again for 5 minutes. Continue this until the Broccolini is charred and crispy, about 20 minutes total. When it's crispy, move the Broccolini to the perimeter of the skillet, add the remaining tablespoon olive oil, and stir in the onion. Cook until the onion is soft and sweet, another 5 minutes, then stir the Broccolini and onions together and, using kitchen scissors, snip everything into 2-inch pieces right in the pan. Remove to a serving platter or bowl and add the desired toppings.

**Makes 4 small plates**

/ vegan /

## Our Favorite Kale Salad with Almonds & Dried Cranberries

If you have time, toss the salad with the dressing about 15 minutes before you eat it. This helps make the kale more tender.

⅔ cup raw almond slivers

1 large bunch curly kale, washed, stems removed and discarded, and finely chopped (about 8 cups)

½ cup dried cranberries

3 tablespoons minced red onion

⅓ cup chopped fresh herbs, preferably dill, chives, and/or parsley

⅔ cups All-Purpose Vinaigrette (page 217), swapping white balsamic vinegar for the red wine vinegar

In a cast-iron pan over medium heat, toast the almonds until roasted and browned, about 3 minutes. Set aside to cool.

In a large serving bowl, toss together the almonds, kale, dried cranberries, onion, herbs, and vinaigrette, preferably 10 to 15 minutes before you want to eat it.

*Makes 4 small plates*

*/ vegan /.*

## Slivered Minty Sugar Snap Peas on a Bed of Ricotta

This is spring on a plate. Whip the ricotta with a whisk or whirl it in a mini food processor if you want a fluffier texture.

8 ounces whole-milk ricotta

¼ cup white wine vinegar

⅓ cup grapeseed oil

Squeeze of honey

Kosher salt and freshly ground black pepper to taste

10 to 12 ounces sugar snap peas, sliced lengthwise, as shown opposite (or chopped however artlessly if you can't deal)

⅓ cup chopped fresh mint leaves

4 small radishes, thinly sliced (optional)

Chili oil to taste

Spread the ricotta on a platter, preferably one with sides, as though you are frosting a cake.

In a medium bowl, whisk together the vinegar, grapeseed oil, honey, salt, and pepper. Toss in the peas, mint, and radishes (if using), coating them thoroughly in the mixture, then pour the vegetables onto the ricotta. Drizzle with chili oil.

*Makes 4 small plates*

# Roasted Beets
# with Herby Yogurt
# & Pistachios

To make this more weeknight friendly, you can buy precooked beets, usually found in the produce section of supermarkets. On the weekend, if I'm going for it, I try to use a multicolored arrangement of beets to optimize the visuals.

2 pounds medium beets (any color), unpeeled, leafy stems removed

3 tablespoons extra-virgin olive oil, plus more for drizzling

1 tablespoon red wine vinegar

Kosher salt and freshly ground black pepper to taste

1 cup full-fat Greek yogurt

¼ cup roughly chopped fresh dill, plus more for serving

¼ cup roughly chopped fresh chives, plus more for serving

2 tablespoons fresh lemon juice

1 garlic clove, pressed

1 teaspoon prepared horseradish

2 tablespoons roasted, salted pistachios, crushed (see page 237 for the how-to)

Preheat the oven to 375°F.

Wrap the beets in foil and bake for 1 hour 30 minutes. Remove from the oven, carefully unwrap them (the steam will be *very* hot), and let the beets cool. Once they are cool enough to handle, remove the skin using your hands. (If your beets are fully cooked, the skins should slip off easily.) Slice the beets into small chunks or coin-size pieces and toss them in a bowl with 1 tablespoon of the olive oil, the red wine vinegar, salt, and pepper. Set aside.

While the beets cook, whirl together the yogurt, dill, chives, lemon juice, garlic, horseradish, and the remaining 2 tablespoons olive oil in a blender or small food processor. The mixture should be on the thick side, but you can add a tablespoon of water if it needs thinning to help blending.

On the bottom of a plate or a shallow bowl, spread the herby yogurt as if you are frosting a cake. (It can be slightly thicker around the edge.) Mound the beets in the center and top with the crushed pistachios, some more dill and chives, and another drizzle of olive oil.

**Makes 4 small plates**

small plates night

# Roasted Eggplant & Tomatoes with Miso-Tahini Sauce

Sharp miso and creamy tahini combine here to elevate regular roasted vegetables to something both indulgent *and* vegan. It is excellent tossed with quinoa or basmati rice if you want to stretch it out for a main dish.

2 pounds Fairy Tale eggplants (halved) or Graffiti eggplants (about 5), cut into 1-inch-thick slices

½ cup extra-virgin olive oil

Kosher salt and freshly ground black pepper to taste

10 to 12 small tomatoes, halved

2 tablespoons tahini

1 teaspoon sweet white miso

½ teaspoon fresh lemon juice

1 teaspoon maple syrup

Leaves from 4 fresh thyme sprigs or chopped fresh flat-leaf parsley

Preheat the oven to 425°F.

In a large bowl, toss the eggplant pieces with the olive oil, salt, and pepper, then place the eggplant in an even single layer on a parchment paper–lined sheet pan. Add the tomatoes to the same large bowl and toss them very gently in whatever oil remains. Nestle the tomatoes in between the eggplant pieces on the sheet pan. Bake for 25 to 30 minutes, until the eggplant looks golden and crispy and the tomatoes are shriveled. Let them cool slightly.

While the vegetables roast, in a jar or small bowl, combine the tahini, miso, lemon juice, maple syrup, and 3 tablespoons water. Cover the jar and shake vigorously to combine, or whisk the ingredients together thoroughly in the bowl.

Transfer the vegetables to a serving bowl, drizzle with tahini-miso sauce, and top with the thyme. Serve warm or at room temperature.

**Makes 4 small plates**

/ vegan /

small plate night

# Greek-Style
# Lemon-Oregano
# Potatoes

I've been making these potatoes (the ultimate hook in our house) ever since first trying the classic Greek dish at the old-school Greek restaurant in Manhattan, Uncle Nick's. I'd argue that you might like them more than french fries—especially when you can find fresh potatoes with golden yellow flesh.

**3 pounds medium Yukon Gold potatoes, peeled and quartered**

**Kosher salt to taste**

**3 tablespoons extra-virgin olive oil, plus more for drizzling**

**¼ cup lemon juice (from 1 medium lemon)**

**2 teaspoons dried oregano**

**Freshly ground black pepper to taste**

Place the potatoes in a medium pot and cover with salted water by 1 inch. Bring to a boil, then decrease heat slightly and aggressively simmer the potatoes for 10 minutes. (They do not have to be fully cooked.) Drain the potatoes.

Meanwhile, preheat the broiler. Line a sheet pan with foil.

Place the drained potatoes on the prepared sheet pan. Drizzle the olive oil all over the potatoes and, using a spoon or your hands, gently toss them to make sure every potato is coated in oil and turned flat-side down. Broil for 8 to 10 minutes, until the potatoes are golden brown. Transfer the potatoes to a serving bowl and toss with the lemon juice, oregano, salt, pepper, and another drizzle of olive oil.

**Makes 4 small plates**

/ *vegan* /

# Andy's Spicy Diced Potatoes

Think of these as the home version of spicy curly fries—with just a hint of heat from the cayenne pepper. I love this recipe, not just because Andy has taken exclusive ownership of it but also because you usually have to parboil potatoes before frying to get really crispy hash browns or fried potatoes. Here, when you dice the potatoes into very small pieces (important!), you can skip that step, saving both time and another pot to wash.

⅓ cup vegetable oil

2 pounds Yukon Gold or red potatoes (important!), peeled and cut into ¼-inch dice

1 tablespoon smoked paprika

1 teaspoon ground cumin

1 teaspoon garlic powder

1 teaspoon onion powder

½ teaspoon cayenne pepper

Kosher salt and freshly ground black pepper to taste

In a very large skillet (you don't want the potatoes to be crowded in the pan, otherwise they will steam rather than crisp up), heat the oil over medium-high heat. Once the oil is hot and shimmery, add the potatoes, then toss in the paprika, cumin, garlic powder, onion powder, cayenne, salt, and black pepper.

Let the potatoes sit, untouched in a single layer, until they brown and crisp on the bottom, about 5 minutes. Stir and let them sit another 5 minutes. Repeat until the potatoes are cooked through and crispy, 20 to 25 minutes total. Serve hot.

**Makes 4 small plates**

/ vegan /

## Brown Butter Corn
## with Parsley

As with all in-season vegetables, you
don't have to do too much to make
peak-season corn taste perfect. In fact,
you don't *want* to do too much, lest you
overwhelm the flavor. I'd argue that
tossing the sweet kernels in a little nutty
brown butter is just the right amount of
interference.

3 tablespoons unsalted butter

Kernels from 4 medium ears
of sweet summer corn

Kosher salt and freshly ground
black pepper to taste

3 tablespoons chopped fresh parsley

Melt the butter in a skillet set over
medium-high heat. Cook until the butter
starts browning and smelling slightly
nutty, about 4 minutes. (You will see
small brown flecks.) Add the corn and
cook, tossing, for 1 minute. Toss with
salt, pepper, and parsley and serve.

**Makes 4 small plates**

## Sesame
## Bok Choy

I love baby bok choy because when
cooked right, the leaves are tender and
the stems retain a delightful crunch.

1 pound baby bok choy

2 tablespoons neutral oil (such as
vegetable or grapeseed oil)

1 teaspoon toasted sesame oil

¼ cup chopped yellow onion

1 garlic clove, minced

1 (1-inch) piece fresh ginger, peeled
and minced (about 1 tablespoon)

Kosher salt and freshly ground black pepper

Chopped scallions, white and
light green parts only

1 tablespoon toasted sesame seeds

Bring a large pot of water to a boil. Add
the bok choy and cook until tender,
about 5 minutes. Drain and return the
pot to the stove.

Over medium heat, add both oils, the
onion, garlic, ginger, salt, and pepper,
stirring until soft and fragrant, about
3 minutes. Toss in the bok choy. Serve
topped with scallions and sesame seeds.

**Makes 4 small plates**

/ vegan /

*small plates night*

## Tomato Salad with Avocado Basil Dressing

Of course, you could toss fresh summer tomatoes with any dressing (see pages 214–217) or with just olive oil, salt, and pepper, and be thrilled. I like this dressing, though, because it's both creamy and completely plant-based.

8 to 10 small fresh basil leaves

1 small avocado, peeled and pitted

2 tablespoons white wine vinegar

⅓ cup extra-virgin olive oil

Kosher salt and freshly ground black pepper to taste

4 or 5 large ripe tomatoes, any variety, preferably heirloom and a mixture of colors, sliced into wedges

2 scallions, light green and white parts only, minced

In a small food processor or blender, combine all but 1 of the basil leaves, the avocado, vinegar, olive oil, salt, pepper, and 2 tablespoons water. Blend until creamy and smooth, about 30 seconds. If it's too thick, add more water, a teaspoon at a time, until the dressing reaches drizzling consistency.

Place the tomato slices on a platter and drizzle the dressing on top. Sprinkle with scallions and serve.

**Makes 4 small plates**

/ vegan /

## Tomato-Nectarine Salad

We've been making this ever since ten-year-old Phoebe went to farm camp and learned how to make tomato-and-nectarine bruschetta. Over the years, we lost the bread, and we try to eat it as often as possible for the brief window when both fruits are at their best.

4 to 5 cups cut fresh, ripe tomatoes, any size or shape, larger tomatoes cut into wedges and smaller tomatoes halved and quartered

1 medium nectarine, pitted and sliced

6 small fresh basil leaves, torn

1 tablespoon finely minced red onion

2 tablespoons white balsamic vinegar

3 tablespoons extra-virgin olive oil

Flaky sea salt, preferably Maldon

Freshly ground black pepper

In a medium bowl, combine the tomatoes, nectarine, basil, and onion. Drizzle the vinegar and olive oil on top, toss, then top with sea salt and a few cranks of black pepper.

**Makes 4 small plates**

/ vegan /

small plates night

## Dill Slaw

We are such slaw people, especially in the winter, when the greens are not so great and we're looking for something fresh and bright on the plate. This one is on repeat in our house—the dill and rice vinegar combination is addictive, it's good on sandwiches (like Crispy Smoky Tofu Sandwiches, page 110), and it's good on its own.

2 teaspoons Dijon mustard

2 tablespoons mayonnaise or vegan or avocado mayonnaise

¼ cup seasoned rice vinegar

⅓ cup extra-virgin olive oil

1 teaspoon sriracha sauce

Kosher salt and freshly ground black pepper to taste

5 cups shredded napa cabbage from a small head

2 tablespoons chopped fresh dill

1 tablespoon minced shallot

In a medium bowl, whisk together the mustard, mayonnaise, rice vinegar, olive oil, sriracha, salt, and pepper. Add the cabbage, dill, and shallot and toss. Let sit for 15 minutes to allow the flavors to meld. Even if you make this in advance, wait until the last 15 minutes before tossing in the dressing so the cabbage retains its crunch.

**Makes 4 small plates**

/ vegan /

## Coconutty Avocado Toasts

Every time I make this for someone, she looks at me quizzically: *What is that taste I'm tasting?* It's coconut oil, and just the smallest bit of it, spread on the toast when it's warm—a trick I learned from my friend and food genius Jen Aaronson—is enough to elevate everybody's favorite Instagram sandwich to something more than basic.

4 thin slices of crusty sourdough bread

2 tablespoons coconut oil (solidified is fine)

2 avocados, halved, pitted, and sliced

*SERVING (OPTIONAL)*

Chopped fresh tomatoes

Chopped fresh cilantro

Fresh sprouts, microgreens, or watercress

Dried red pepper flakes

Seven-Minute Eggs (page 197; omit for vegans)

"Everything bagel" seasoning

Toast the bread. Immediately spread coconut oil on the toasts while they are still warm. Lay overlapping slices of avocado on each piece of toast, then slightly mash them so the slices meld together. Top as desired and serve.

**Makes 4 toasts**

/ vegan /

# Roasted Honeynut Squash with Crispy Sage Leaves

Sage will always remind me of Thanksgiving stuffing, but here it's given the star treatment, crisped up in oil and salted so the leaves taste as addictive as potato chips. I'm not kidding. Make extra because they'll disappear as you cook them, thanks to curious, meddling snackers casually walking by.

4 cups peeled and (1-inch) cubed honeynut or butternut squash (about 20 ounces)

5 tablespoons extra-virgin olive oil

Kosher salt and freshly ground black pepper to taste

15 to 20 fresh small to medium sage leaves

Preheat the oven to 425°F. Line a sheet pan with foil.

Place the squash cubes on the prepared sheet pan and toss with 3 tablespoons of the olive oil, salt, and pepper. Roast until golden and crispy around the edges, 20 to 25 minutes, tossing halfway through.

Meanwhile, in a small cast-iron skillet, heat the remaining 2 tablespoons olive oil over high heat. Pan-fry the sage leaves in batches (3 or 4 at a time), flipping them after about 15 seconds with tongs. (They should sizzle and shrink slightly; that's how you know the pan is hot enough.) Remove to a paper-towel-lined plate, sprinkle with salt immediately, and try not to eat them like potato chips. Repeat with the remaining sage leaves. Serve the roasted squash topped with the fried sage leaves (you can crumble them if you like) and more salt and pepper.

Makes 4 small plates

/ vegan /

## Restuffed Japanese Sweet Potatoes with Miso & Chives

Japanese sweet potatoes, also known as Murasaki potatoes, look like sweet potatoes on the outside, but their skins are deeper magenta and their creamy yellowish flesh is lighter and less cloyingly sweet than regular ones. When paired with miso—which they commonly are—you have a rich-salty hit to contrast with the sweet creaminess. Also, the skin is edible, so when it gets crispy, you can eat the whole thing with your hands and it will feel almost like you're eating an ice cream cone. Note: To get the potatoes super creamy, whirl them in a food processor instead of using a masher.

4 Japanese sweet potatoes
(approximately 4 [10-ounce] potatoes)

4 tablespoons (½ stick) unsalted
butter, chopped roughly into pieces

2 tablespoons sweet white miso

¼ cup chopped fresh chives

Kosher salt and freshly ground
black pepper to taste

Preheat the oven to 425°F.

Bake the potatoes until the skins feel loose and slightly crispy, 45 to 50 minutes. While they are baking, add the butter and miso to a medium bowl and mash together with a fork. Remove the potatoes from the oven and split each one lengthwise, holding the potatoes with an oven mitt or kitchen towel because they'll be very hot. Let them cool slightly, then scoop out the flesh from each half into the bowl with the butter and miso, mashing everything with a fork or a potato masher until well blended. Spoon the filling back into each half and garnish with chives, salt, and pepper.

**Serves 4**

# a vegetarian special bag of & tricks

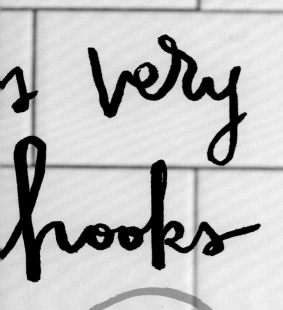

*very hooks*

RECIPES THAT CAST A GLOW OF EXCITEMENT OVER ANYTHING NEXT TO THEM ON THE PLATE

# PROTEIN HITS

———

Before I started limiting meat, I, like a lot of cooks,
tended to use animal proteins as a starting point for dinner.
*I have a pork tenderloin, I'll pan-roast and serve it with apples
and potatoes. I have a piece of salmon, I'll grill and serve it with
ginger-scallion sauce and Brussels sprouts.* When strategizing
about vegetarian dinners, it's become the opposite. Usually,
I'll have something in mind, like a grain bowl or a salad
or a pizza, and think, *How can I add a protein hit to dinner
tonight?* It's a common obstacle for people who want to
go vegetarian—here are a few easy strategies to help.

196

the vegetarian's very special bag of hooks & tricks

## Seven-Minute Eggs

Sure, you can top your rice bowls and salads with hard-boiled or fried eggs, but there's something just a little more enticing about a seven-minute one, all jammy and pretty when cooked just right.

**4 large eggs**

Bring a medium pot of water to a boil. Using a slotted spoon, carefully lower the eggs into the water, turning the heat down slightly so the boil is controlled and not aggressive. Set your timer for 7 minutes, not a second more or less. While the eggs are simmering, prepare an ice bath by filling a bowl large enough to fit your eggs with ice and water. When your timer goes off, immediately transfer the eggs into the ice bath. Remove after a minute or two (I don't love freezing-cold eggs) and peel gently.

Makes 4 eggs

USE ON TOP OF

A FARROTTA FOR ALL SEASONS (PAGE 50)

COCONUTTY AVOCADO TOASTS (PAGE 187)

PEPPERY SPROUT SALAD WITH AVOCADO (PAGE 170)

CHICKPEA CAESAR SALAD (PAGE 69)

## Basic Baked Tofu

The tofu technique that converted all the haters in my house was the kind where you fry cornstarch-dredged cubes in a hot pan with oil, then toss them in a sweet and spicy glaze (like the Sweet-Hot Chili Glaze, page 210, the Spicy Peanut Sauce, page 203, or a basic Teriyaki Sauce, page 211). I find this technique for roasting is less messy and yet still yields a nice crispy cube. It's the one I fall back on 99 percent of the time I'm eating tofu for dinner, especially when dinner is salad and I'm looking for a quick protein add-in.

**1 (14- to 15-ounce) block extra-firm tofu, pressed, drained, and cut into ½-inch cubes (see page 237)**

**3 tablespoons neutral oil, such as vegetable or grapeseed oil, or extra-virgin olive oil**

**2 tablespoons soy sauce**

**1 tablespoon cornstarch**

**¼ teaspoon cayenne pepper (optional)**

Preheat the oven to 425°F. Line a sheet pan with parchment paper.

In a bowl, toss the tofu with the oil, soy sauce, cornstarch, and cayenne (if using) and place on the prepared sheet pan. Bake until the tofu is golden and the corners look crispy, about 20 minutes.

Makes 3 cups cubed cooked tofu

USE IN

EGGPLANT & TOFU WITH SWEET-HOT CHILI GLAZE (PAGE 55)

WHEAT BERRIES WITH CRISPY TOFU, GRAPES, ARUGULA & FETA (PAGE 62)

CABBAGE-KALE-TOFU SALAD WITH CITRUSY GINGER DRESSING (PAGE 65)

/ vegan /

# Crispy Chickpeas

I'm giving you two methods of preparation because I go back and forth depending on how many pots and oven racks are being used for the rest of dinner. While I prefer the stovetop version (easier to monitor), you can use the methods interchangeably. (Though you'll probably want to use the roasting method if you don't have a skillet large enough to fry the chickpeas in one layer.) I'd recommend committing both to memory—you'll be making them a lot. Either way, be sure to dry the rinsed and drained chickpeas on paper towels or a kitchen towel as much as possible before cooking them. Also, to get maximum crispiness, you'll want to eat the chickpeas within a few hours of making them, optimally right away.

⅓ cup vegetable oil or extra-virgin olive oil

3 cups cooked chickpeas, or
2 (15-ounce) cans, rinsed and drained

Kosher salt and freshly ground
black pepper to taste

Optional spice mixture: ¼ teaspoon
smoked paprika, ¼ teaspoon garlic
powder, ⅛ teaspoon cayenne

**ROASTING METHOD:** Preheat the oven to 450°F. Line a sheet pan with foil.

Make the spice mixture, if using, by combining the paprika, garlic powder, and cayenne in a small bowl.

Toss the oil and chickpeas together on the prepared sheet pan. (I use my hands to make sure they are all evenly coated.) Roast for 30 minutes, until the chickpeas are crispy. Transfer the chickpeas to a paper-towel-lined bowl and lightly blot any excess oil. Slip the paper towel out of the bowl, then toss the crispy chickpeas with a few pinches of salt, black pepper, and spice mixture (if using).

**FRYING METHOD:** Make the spice mixture, if using, by combining the paprika, garlic powder, and cayenne in a small bowl.

Add the oil to a large skillet or Dutch oven set over medium-high heat. (You want the pan or pot to be large enough to hold the chickpeas in a single layer; otherwise use two skillets or cook in batches if you have time.) When the oil is hot but not smoking, add the chickpeas. Fry for 12 to 15 minutes, until slightly shriveled and crispy looking, tossing with a slotted spoon every 5 minutes. (Resist the urge to stir; let them sit and get crispy.) Using the slotted spoon, transfer the chickpeas to a paper-towel-lined platter to briefly drain; then, while still hot, place them in a medium bowl and toss with the salt, black pepper, and spice mixture (if using).

Makes 3 cups

USE IN

CHICKPEA CAESAR SALAD (PAGE 69)

BARLEY BOWLS WITH CHICKPEAS, ROASTED
VEGETABLES & AVOCADO DRESSING (PAGE 49)

CRISPY CHICKPEAS WITH NAAN &
YOGURT SAUCE (PAGE 198)

/ vegan /

# MAGIC BLENDER SAUCES & DRESSINGS

There was a time in my weeknight cooking life when,
if I came across the phrase "In your food processor..." in a recipe,
I would automatically turn the page. And yet now I use the
thing almost every day. Why the turnaround? I can't help
noticing the correlation between the food processor's frequency
of use and an increase in our vegetarian cooking. These days,
when I'm missing the depth of flavor that comes from, say, a piece
of bacon, my mind hurtles in the direction of... sauce. A bright,
tangy salsa for tacos; an herby, creamy ranch dressing for crisp
summer vegetables; a decadent peanut sauce for noodles, steamed
vegetables, or slaw; a cool, sharp Caesar that can make even a
piece of shoe leather appetizing. Aren't you getting hungry?

the vegetarian's very special bag of hooks & tricks

## Tomatillo Sauce

The ease with which this can be made is completely disproportionate to the depth it brings to a dish. Bright, fresh, and tangy, it's a dramatic upgrade from its widely available store-bought counterparts.

- 10 small tomatillos, husks removed
- 1 jalapeño pepper, stemmed, seeded, and ribs removed
- 1 medium garlic clove, chopped
- 2 cups loosely packed fresh cilantro, both tender stems and leaves, roughly chopped
- 2 tablespoons chopped white onion
- Kosher salt and freshly ground black pepper to taste

In a small saucepan, cover the tomatillos and the jalapeño with water. Bring to a boil, then lower to an aggressive simmer and cook for 10 minutes. Strain, discarding the liquid, and whirl the mixture in a food processor or blender along with the garlic, cilantro, onion, salt, and black pepper until it reaches a sauce-like consistency.

Makes 2½ cups

*USE IN*

GREEN ENCHILADAS WITH
TOMATILLO SAUCE (PAGE 105)

ALONGSIDE MIGAS TACOS (PAGE 97)

*Store in the refrigerator, covered, for up to 5 days.*

/ vegan /

## Spicy Peanut Sauce

I have been addicted to this sauce ever since my first bowl of goma-ae, the Japanese side dish made with steamed vegetables (usually spinach) and drizzled with peanut sauce. It almost feels like cheating it's so delicious.

- 1 small garlic clove, roughly chopped
- 1 (1-inch) piece fresh ginger, peeled and roughly chopped
- ½ cup smooth peanut butter (commercial or natural style)
- ⅓ cup warm water, plus more as needed
- 2 tablespoons soy sauce
- 1 tablespoon toasted sesame oil
- 1 tablespoon red wine vinegar or apple cider vinegar
- 1 teaspoon sugar
- 4 or 5 drops hot sauce

Combine the garlic, ginger, peanut butter, warm water, soy sauce, sesame oil, vinegar, sugar, and hot sauce in a blender or a small food processor and process until smooth. Add more warm water if it is on the thick side. (You want it to be more saucy than dippy.)

Makes 1 cup

*USE IN*

TOFU WITH BROCCOLI & SPICY
PEANUT SAUCE (PAGE 133)

STEAMED KALE WITH SPICY
PEANUT SAUCE (PAGE 172)

AS A DIP FOR VEGETABLES

TOSSED WITH COOKED THIN SPAGHETTI,
CUCUMBERS, AND SCALLIONS FOR
CLASSIC COLD SESAME NOODLES

*Store in the refrigerator, covered, for up to 1 week.*

/ vegan /

# Caesar Dressing

I can't overstate how a good homemade Caesar dressing has the power to rewrite the narrative on the probably hundreds of sad, flavorless versions you've eaten in your lifetime. My first version here forgoes the customary raw egg in favor of mayonnaise, a trick I learned from cookbook author Julia Turshen that somehow makes things psychologically easier without compromising any flavor. The second, a vegan take, leans on the salty umami of nutritional yeast to achieve the same addictive bite. I honestly can't say which one I like better. Also, as my sixteen-year-old Caesar addict once observed, just because Caesar salad is *called* Caesar salad doesn't mean it should have exclusive rights to its use. I agree. Use this with abandon atop all your favorite salads.

**204**

1 small garlic clove, minced

½ teaspoon Dijon mustard

1 tablespoon fresh lemon juice

1 tablespoon white wine vinegar

¼ cup extra-virgin olive oil

2 heaping tablespoons mayonnaise

3 tablespoons grated Parmesan cheese

Kosher salt and freshly ground black pepper to taste

In a blender or food processor, puree the garlic, mustard, lemon juice, vinegar, olive oil, and mayonnaise until smooth. Add the Parmesan and give the dressing a few pulses just to incorporate the cheese. Season with salt and pepper.

Makes ⅔ cup

USE IN

CHICKPEA CAESAR SALAD (PAGE 69)

ANY GREEN SALAD

*Store in the refrigerator, covered, for up to 1 week.*

the vegetarian's very special bag of hooks & tricks

## No-Blender Vegan Caesar Dressing

2 teaspoons Dijon mustard

3 tablespoons white wine vinegar

1 tablespoon fresh lemon juice
(from ½ small lemon)

2 tablespoons vegan mayonnaise
or cashew cream (see sidebar)

2 tablespoons nutritional yeast

¼ cup extra-virgin olive oil

Kosher salt and freshly ground
black pepper to taste

In a jar or small bowl, combine the mustard, vinegar, lemon juice, vegan mayonnaise, nutritional yeast, olive oil, a few pinches each of salt and pepper, and 1 tablespoon water. Cover the jar and shake vigorously to combine, or whisk the ingredients together thoroughly in the bowl. Add more water, if needed, to thin the dressing.

Makes ⅔ cup

USE

WHEREVER YOU USE CAESAR DRESSING

Store in the refrigerator, covered,
for up to 1 week.

. . . . . . . . . . . . . . . . . . . . . . . . .

### HOMEMADE CASHEW CREAM
*Soak 1 cup raw cashews in enough water to cover for at least 30 minutes and up to 1 day. Add the soaked cashews to a blender with the liquid and whirl until it's creamy and thick, about 30 seconds; I like it a little looser than almond butter. Makes 1 cup. Store in the refrigerator, covered, for up to 4 days.*

. . . . . . . . . . . . . . . . . . . . . . . . .

206

## Cilantro Pesto

I love the brightness of this pesto (in both color and taste) and how, unlike those of most herbs, the stems of the cilantro are tender and flavorful, so you can just throw them washed into the blender without the fussy step of trimming and removing leaves.

1 cup fresh cilantro leaves and tender stems

½ cup extra-virgin olive oil

¼ cup roasted pepitas (pumpkin seeds)

1 tablespoon fresh lime juice (from ½ lime)

Kosher salt and freshly ground black pepper to taste

Dash of hot sauce

Combine the cilantro, olive oil, pepitas, lime juice, salt, pepper, and hot sauce in a mini food processor or blender until it reaches pesto consistency, scraping down the sides of the processor as necessary.

Makes ¾ cup

USE IN

ROASTED BUTTERNUT SQUASH & BLACK BEAN TACOS (PAGE 101)

MIGAS TACOS (PAGE 97)

DRIZZLED ON SCRAMBLED EGGS

TOSSED WITH FRESH TOMATOES OR ROASTED BEETS

*Store in the refrigerator, covered, for up to 1 week.*

/ vegan /

## Kale Pesto

This recipe is great to have on hand when you are confronted with a bunch of end-of-the-week kale that is about to go bad. I use almonds here for a practical reason—unlike pine nuts, which are typically used in basil pesto, I almost always have almonds in the pantry (for snacking, for making granola, etc.). The result is a milder and grassier pesto. You can absolutely swap in the traditional pine nuts (and the basil) if you have those on hand.

Kosher salt to taste

4 cups torn curly kale, tough stems removed

½ large clove garlic, roughly chopped

3 tablespoons grated Parmesan cheese

Freshly ground black pepper to taste

¼ cup raw blanched almonds

3 tablespoons fresh lemon juice (from 1 small lemon)

½ teaspoon honey

⅓ cup extra-virgin olive oil

Make an ice bath by filling a medium bowl with ice and water. Bring a large pot of salted water to a boil and add the kale. Cook until wilted and softened, about 2½ minutes. Reserve ⅓ cup of the cooking water and, using tongs or a slotted spoon, transfer the kale to the ice bath to stop the cooking process and preserve its bright green color. Drain and cool until the leaves are comfortable to handle. Place the leaves between two paper towels and wring out as much moisture as you can.

In a blender or a food processor, pulse the blanched kale, garlic, Parmesan, salt, pepper, almonds, and 2 tablespoons of the lemon juice until coarsely chopped. Add the honey and olive oil and continue to pulse. Taste and adjust with the remaining 1 tablespoon lemon juice or the reserved kale water (if you prefer a less tangy flavor) until the pesto reaches a drizzling consistency.

**Makes ¾ cup**

*USE IN*

*THE GREENEST PASTA (SPAGHETTI WITH PEAS, BROCCOLINI & KALE PESTO, PAGE 92)*

*DOLLOPED ON EASIEST WHITE BEAN SOUP (PAGE 78)*

*DRIZZLED OVER BURRATA ALONGSIDE CROSTINI AND SUMMER VEGETABLES*

*Store in the refrigerator, covered, for up to 1 week.*

## Yogurt-Harissa Sauce

One thing that hasn't changed with our new cooking routine is our love of heat, and at all times you can find a fleet of hot sauces and chili pastes from around the world in our refrigerator door waiting to be deployed, like sriracha, gochujang, sambal oelek, and harissa. The shortcut lover in me has a particular affinity for harissa—originally from Tunisia, it's popular across many North African cuisines—because it's spiced, so even a few teaspoons, like in this recipe, lend not just heat but an intense depth of flavor with hints of coriander, fennel, and allspice.

⅓ cup plain Greek yogurt (2% or full fat)

3 tablespoons extra-virgin olive oil

2 teaspoons harissa paste

2 tablespoons red wine vinegar

Kosher salt and freshly ground
black pepper to taste

¼ cup chopped fresh dill

1 clove garlic, chopped

1 tablespoon fresh lemon juice
(from ½ small lemon)

½ teaspoon honey

In a blender or mini food processor, process the yogurt, olive oil, harissa, vinegar, salt, pepper, dill, garlic, lemon juice, and honey until the mixture is thick, like a creamy salad dressing. (If you feel it's too thick, add 1 tablespoon of water at a time until you get to your preferred consistency.)

Makes ⅔ cup

*USE IN*

SHREDDED CARROT SALAD WITH
YOGURT-HARISSA SAUCE (PAGE 170)

ALONGSIDE ANY-WHICH-WAY CHOPPED,
CHARRED BROCCOLINI (PAGE 173)

AS A DIP FOR YOGURT FLATBREAD (PAGE 222)

*Store in the refrigerator, covered,
for up to 1 week.*

the vegetarian's very special bag of hooks & tricks

## Salsa Fresca

For most of the year, the salsa in our house comes straight from the jar. But for the few weeks in late summer and early fall when the tomatoes are at their best, I make this fresh one as often as I can, because it transforms even the most basic quesadilla or bowl of chips from a ho-hum, everyday kind of dish to a fresh, bright, special one. Two things to note: First, if you are not morally opposed to purchasing grape tomatoes outside of tomato season, tossing a few chopped fresh ones with your jarred salsa is a fast, easy cheat for the rest of the year. Second, if circumstances allow, make this ahead of time and chill, which really allows the flavors to meld.

2½ cups finely diced fresh tomatoes (the freshest you can find), preferably heirloom, with juices

¼ cup chopped fresh cilantro, leaves and stems

1 small garlic clove, pressed or finely minced

2 tablespoons finely minced sweet white onion

½ small jalapeño pepper, stemmed, seeded, and ribs removed

1 tablespoon red wine vinegar

1 tablespoon extra-virgin olive oil

Kosher salt and freshly ground black pepper to taste

Dash of hot sauce

In a medium bowl, combine the tomatoes, cilantro, garlic, onion, jalapeño, vinegar, olive oil, salt, black pepper, and hot sauce. Stir everything together and taste for heat. Add a few more drops of hot sauce if desired.

Makes 2½ cups

USE IN

ANDY'S SUNDAY ENCHILADAS WITH RED SAUCE (PAGE 106)

MIGAS TACOS (PAGE 97)

ALONGSIDE CHICKPEA-PASTA MAC & CHEESE WITH CHOPPED TOMATOES (PAGE 88)

WITH CHIPS

*Store in the refrigerator, covered, for 5 to 7 days.*

/ vegan /

# Sweet-Hot Chili Glaze

A few years ago, after a day hiking around the Shenandoah Valley, we somehow stumbled upon the best broccoli of our lives at a Staunton, Virginia, restaurant called Zynodoa. Sweet and hot, crunchy and spicy, it was called Crispy Glazed Broccoli. We loved it so much we made them give us the recipe so we could attempt it ourselves at home. We simplified their version, which called for sorghum molasses and benne seeds, and pretty soon the glaze found its way onto other roasted vegetables (especially Brussels sprouts) and tossed into stir-fries. Warning: It's definitely for people who like a little heat.

**3 tablespoons hot chili sauce (such as Cholula or Pete's brand)**

**2 tablespoons honey**

**2 tablespoons packed light brown sugar**

**Kosher salt to taste**

**4 tablespoons (½ stick) unsalted butter, cut into small cubes**

**Freshly ground black pepper to taste**

In a small saucepan set over medium heat, combine the hot chili sauce, honey, brown sugar, and salt and simmer until the sugar has dissolved completely. Remove the pan from the heat and while the mixture is hot, whisk in the butter to thicken the sauce. Season with salt and pepper.

**Makes ⅓ cup**

*USE IN*

*EGGPLANT & TOFU WITH SWEET-HOT CHILI GLAZE (PAGE 55)*

*TOSSED WITH BASIC BAKED TOFU (PAGE 197), OR ANY-WHICH-WAY CHOPPED, CHARRED BROCCOLINI (PAGE 173)*

*TOSSED WITH ROASTED BRUSSELS SPROUTS*

*Store in the refrigerator, covered, for 5 to 7 days.*

the vegetarian's very special bag of hooks & tricks

# Teriyaki Sauce

The word *teriyaki* in Japan refers to a technique—grilling and basting something (meat usually) with a sweet soy-sauce-and-mirin-based marinade. In my house, though, it means one thing: clean plates. During a particularly frustrating picky-eater phase, we discovered that a bottled version of teriyaki sauce was even more effective than ketchup in terms of convincing Abby to eat a piece of fish or a stalk of roasted broccoli. We went through so much of it that I was forced to learn how to scare up a from-scratch version when we'd run dry. And while there is only one recipe in this book that calls specifically for this glaze (Teriyaki-Glazed Crispy Tofu with Green Beans), I've been known to put it on literally anything in my house (roast Brussels sprouts or broccoli, warm rice, Seven-Minute Eggs, page 197), and it reliably guarantees a spark of happy recognition.

½ cup soy sauce

¼ cup mirin

3 tablespoons light brown sugar

1 tablespoon honey

1 clove garlic, halved

1 tablespoon cornstarch

In a small saucepan, whisk together the soy sauce, mirin, ¼ cup water, the brown sugar, honey, and garlic. Heat on medium-low until the sugar dissolves, about 3 minutes, stirring occasionally.

Meanwhile, in a small bowl, mix the cornstarch with 2 tablespoons water until smooth, then whisk it into the sauce. Continue to cook until the sauce simmers slightly and thickens, about another minute. If you're using the teriyaki right away, remove the garlic halves; if not, store the sauce in a jar with the garlic (remember to remove the garlic before using).

Makes 1 cup

USE IN

TERIYAKI-GLAZED CRISPY TOFU
WITH GREEN BEANS (PAGE 135)

TOSSED WITH ROASTED BROCCOLI,
CARAMELIZED ONIONS, OR ANY FOOD YOU ARE
TRYING TO CONVINCE A SKEPTIC TO EAT

*Store in the refrigerator, covered,
for 3 to 5 days.*

# DRESSINGS THAT ARE ALWAYS ON STANDBY

When I have bottles of these dressings in the house—
ready to be tossed into green salads and grain salads
or drizzled over tofu or roast vegetables—I call it
"money in the bank." Even if it's the only homemade
thing on the plate, dinner's going to taste good.

the vegetarian's very special bag of hooks & tricks

## Miso-Tahini Sauce

I use this vegan dressing when I want creaminess without the cream (tahini) and umami without the Parmesan (miso).

3 tablespoons tahini

2 teaspoons sweet white miso

1 teaspoon lemon juice

2 teaspoons maple syrup

In a jar or small bowl, combine the tahini, miso, lemon juice, and maple syrup with ⅓ cup water. Cover the jar and shake vigorously to combine, or whisk the ingredients together thoroughly in the bowl until creamy and emulsified; the mixture should have a pourable consistency.

Makes ¾ cup

USE IN

ROASTED EGGPLANT & TOMATOES WITH MISO-TAHINI SAUCE (PAGE 178)

DRIZZLED ON BAKED SWEET POTATOES OR BUTTERNUT SQUASH

AS A DRESSING FOR SIMPLE GREEN OR GRAIN SALADS

*Store in the refrigerator, covered, for up to 1 week, shaking or whisking again before using.*

 / vegan /

## Pizza Dressing

I grew up pouring this onto salads and sesame-seed-crusted bread at Italian restaurants with red-checkered tablecloths. My kids grew up with it tossed with salad greens that topped tomato pizzas. It's homey, nostalgic, and as simple as it gets.

¼ cup red wine vinegar

⅓ cup extra-virgin olive oil

2 teaspoons dried oregano

Kosher salt and freshly ground black pepper to taste

In a jar or medium bowl, combine the vinegar, olive oil, oregano, salt, and pepper. Cover the jar and shake vigorously, or whisk the ingredients together thoroughly in the bowl until emulsified.

Makes about ½ cup

USE IN

PIZZA SALAD WITH WHITE BEANS (PAGE 66)

TOSSED WITH FRESH TOMATOES

DRIZZLED ON A DELI-STYLE SANDWICH WEDGE OF MOZZARELLA (OR PROVOLONE), GREENS, SPROUTS, TOMATOES, AND AVOCADO

*Store in the refrigerator, covered, for up to 1 week, shaking or whisking again before using.*

# Herby Buttermilk Ranch

This dressing—somehow simultaneously decadent, creamy, tangy, and bright—is always the second thing I think to make when I have leftover buttermilk. (First thing: pancakes, natch.)

2 tablespoons fresh lemon juice
(from 1 medium lemon)

2 teaspoons Dijon mustard

1 teaspoon garlic powder

Kosher salt and freshly ground
black pepper to taste

2 tablespoons chopped shallot
or red onion

2 tablespoons chopped
fresh flat-leaf parsley

2 tablespoons chopped fresh dill

2 tablespoons chopped fresh chives

¼ cup extra-virgin olive oil

½ cup buttermilk

In a jar or medium bowl, combine the lemon juice, mustard, garlic powder, salt, pepper, shallot, parsley, dill, chives, olive oil, and buttermilk. Cover the jar and shake vigorously to combine, or whisk the ingredients together thoroughly in the bowl until creamy and emulsified.

Makes ¾ cup

*USE IN*

BROILED CAESAR SALAD WITH
CHICKPEAS (PAGE 69)

SWAPPED FOR THE ROMESCO
UNDERNEATH CAULIFLOWER CUTLETS
WITH ROMESCO SAUCE (PAGE 144)

AS A DIP FOR RAW VEGETABLES

IN THE CAVITY OF A HOLLOWED-OUT AVOCADO
FOR A QUICK SNACK OR EASY SIDE DISH

*Store in the refrigerator, covered,
for up to 1 week, shaking or
whisking again before using.*

the vegetarian's very special bag of hooks & tricks

# All-Purpose Vinaigrette

If you've been cooking for even a few years, chances are you have your own all-purpose dressing—the one you make on autopilot for any salad, whether greens-based, bean-based, or grain-based. I choose the vinegar depending on mood and dish (though I'd say red wine vinegar probably tops the leader board here) and often keep the same jar going in the refrigerator for weeks at a time, filling and refilling, building on what's left and mixing in new herbs and seasonings. I recommend memorizing the recipe. Nothing will feel more useful (and upgrade a dinner faster) than homemade dressing ready to go. Note: For a creamier version, mix in 1 tablespoon of mayonnaise.

**1 tablespoon Dijon mustard**

**¼ cup vinegar, such as red wine, white wine, or white balsamic vinegar**

**1 tablespoon fresh lemon juice**

**½ teaspoon sugar or honey**

**Kosher salt and freshly ground black pepper to taste**

**1 tablespoon chopped fresh herbs, such as parsley, chives, tarragon, or basil (optional)**

**½ cup extra-virgin olive oil**

In a small jar or measuring cup, combine the mustard, vinegar, lemon juice, sugar, salt, pepper, and herbs (if using). Cover the jar and shake vigorously to combine, or whisk the ingredients together in the measuring cup. Add the olive oil and shake (or whisk) again until the mixture is emulsified.

Makes ⅔ cup

*USE IN*

*OUR FAVORITE KALE SALAD WITH ALMONDS & DRIED CRANBERRIES (PAGE 174)*

*QUINOA WITH ROASTED WINTER VEGETABLES (PAGE 61)*

*ON ANY GREEN, BEAN, OR GRAIN SALAD*

*Store in the refrigerator, covered, for up to 1 week, shaking or whisking again before using.*

# BREAD MAKES EVERYTHING BETTER

~~~~~~~~~

There is a grand tradition in my family not of bread
*baking* but of bread *buying*. In the 1940s, my grandfather, on
the way home from his work as a tailor in New York's
Garment District, would swing by his neighborhood Bronx
bakery and pick up baguettes and a challah for dinner. My
father carried on the tradition with his family, always
walking through our back screen door cradling a
fresh-baked loaf like it was a newborn, something
Andy also started doing when we first moved in together
in mid-1990s Brooklyn. Me? I frequently do the same—
thanks to them, today, nothing anchors the meal and says
"family" louder to me than fresh-baked bread—but when I
can't, I rely on quick breads and these hacks, hints, and hits.

# Za'atar Pizza Dough Flatbread

Za'atar is an actual wild herb, but it also refers to a toasty, herby, zesty mixture made from Middle Eastern spices, some combination of za'atar, dried thyme, oregano, sumac, and toasted sesame seeds. One night, when I was in search of a "hook" to serve with a basic salad, I sprinkled a few tablespoons of the mixture onto rolled-out store-bought pizza dough, dimpling the dough like a focaccia and pricking it to prevent big air bubbles. Fifteen minutes later it was on the table, still warm, with olive oil for dipping.

**3 tablespoons extra-virgin olive oil**

**1 (16-ounce) pizza dough (store-bought is fine), at room temperature for at least 30 minutes and up to 3 hours (this makes it easier to work with)**

**¼ teaspoon garlic powder**

**2 tablespoons za'atar**

Preheat the oven to 450°F. Grease a sheet pan with 1 tablespoon of the olive oil and set the dough on top. Use your fingers to press the dough so it stretches out almost to the corners of the pan. It's OK if it's a little thick. (This is not thin-crust pizza you are making.) Using your fingers, create a few dimples in the surface, then take a fork and prick it a half-dozen times.

In a small bowl, mix together the remaining 2 tablespoons olive oil and the garlic powder and brush the top of the dough. Sprinkle the za'atar all over the dough and bake until golden and puffy, 10 to 15 minutes. Remove and cut into strips or wedges. Serve warm.

Serves 6 to 8

*USE WITH*

THE CREAMIEST HUMMUS (PAGE 164)

STEWY BLACK LENTILS WITH
CHARD & FETA (PAGE 77)

UNDERNEATH SOME CHOPPED
SEVEN-MINUTE EGGS (PAGE 197)

ALONGSIDE ANY SALAD OR BOWL
OF FRESH VEGETABLES

the vegetarian's very special bag of hooks & tricks

# Yogurt Flatbread

You might not want to make this naan-like quick bread on the kind of night when you've missed your regular train or a kid has a late soccer practice way across the county. It's not hard, per se, but it does involve some concentration and 20 minutes of sitting-around time, two things you probably might not associate with the word *weeknight*. If you do have a few more minutes than usual, though, you'll be so thankful. Tender and tangy, it elicits actual tableside cheers every time.

1½ cups all-purpose or white whole-wheat flour, plus extra for rolling

2 teaspoons baking powder

¼ teaspoon kosher salt

1¼ cups plain whole-milk Greek yogurt

2 tablespoons extra-virgin olive oil

In a large bowl and using a wooden spoon, mix together the flour, baking powder, salt, and yogurt until a moist, shaggy dough forms. Then, using your hands, knead the dough right in the bowl until it's smooth. This should take about 2 minutes.

Divide the dough into 4 equal portions, roll each into a ball on a lightly floured surface, and set them on a dinner plate or the counter. Cover the dough balls loosely with a kitchen towel and let them rest for 20 minutes, until they are slightly puffier.

Lightly flour your work surface and set a dough ball on top. Using a rolling pin, roll the dough into an 8-inch round, dusting the work surface and the dough with more flour as needed.

Set a 10- or 12-inch cast-iron skillet over medium-high heat for about 2 minutes. Add about ½ tablespoon of olive oil (enough to very thinly coat the bottom) and place a rolled-out piece of dough in the pan. Cook until it's bubbly and golden brown, about 2 minutes, then flip and repeat on the second side. Remove the bread to a plate and tent with foil to keep warm. Repeat with the remaining balls of dough, brushing the pan with more oil as needed. Reheat any leftovers in the toaster oven.

**Makes 4 flatbreads**

USE WITH

THE CREAMIEST HUMMUS (PAGE 164)

IN PLACE OF NAAN IN CRISPY CHICKPEAS WITH NAAN & YOGURT SAUCE (PAGE 140)

ALONGSIDE SHREDDED CARROT SALAD WITH YOGURT-HARISSA SAUCE (PAGE 170) OR HOT HONEY BRUSSELS SPROUTS (PAGE 172)

*the vegetarian's very special bag of hooks & tricks*

## Honey-Crusted Skillet Corn Bread

The prep here is actually no more complicated than mixing up a bowl of pancake batter, and I dare you not to be excited about dinner when there is a piece of warm, buttery corn bread waiting for you. The honey and butter—cooked first in the skillet, creating a deep, textured caramelized crust—is a revelation here, taking everyday corn bread from good to great.

10 tablespoons (1¼ sticks) unsalted butter

⅓ cup plus 1 tablespoon sugar

1 cup cornmeal

1 cup all-purpose flour

2½ teaspoons baking powder

¼ teaspoon kosher salt

1 cup buttermilk

1 egg, lightly beaten

1 tablespoon honey

Flaky sea salt, preferably Maldon, for sprinkling

Preheat the oven to 400°F. Arrange a rack in the middle of the oven.

In a small saucepan, melt 9 tablespoons of the butter. In a large bowl, stir together ⅓ cup of the sugar, the cornmeal, flour, baking powder, and kosher salt. Gently mix in the melted butter, buttermilk, and egg.

Set an 8- or 9-inch cast-iron skillet over medium heat. Add the remaining 1 tablespoon butter to the pan. Once it melts, sprinkle the remaining 1 tablespoon sugar and drizzle the honey all over the skillet's surface. Let it cook for 2 minutes, until it sizzles and looks slightly golden brown. Remove from the heat.

Using a rubber spatula, scrape the batter into the skillet, sprinkle with sea salt, and bake for 25 minutes. The corn bread is done when the edges are lightly browned and a knife inserted in the center comes out clean. Cut into 3-inch pieces and serve. Store leftovers in a covered container or BPA-free, zip-top plastic bag for up to 3 days. To reheat later, wrap the squares in foil and warm in a 300°F oven for 20 minutes.

*Makes 9 pieces*

*USE WITH*

*THREE-BEAN CHILI BOWLS WITH CHOCOLATE & PLANTAIN CHIPS (PAGE 46)*

*SPICY-TANGY-SMOKY PINTO BEAN BOWLS (PAGE 52)*

*(IF YOU HAVE LEFTOVERS) ALONGSIDE CHOPPED BROCCOLINI SALAD WITH DILL & FETA (PAGE 173) FOR THE NEXT DAY'S LUNCH*

*the vegetarian's very special bag of hooks & tricks*

# Hand-Torn Croutons

Once you discover homemade croutons, you'll be so happy to have stale bread lying around. I love tearing the bread artlessly into different shapes, so the pieces are all craggy—it's easier than chopping it into uniform cubes and ideal for soaking up dressings, adding texture, and looking rustic and fun. Warning: Do not let the croutons cool where a passerby can reach them, or you will have none left for dinner. Lastly: Feel free to skip the mixing bowl (one less thing to wash) and toss everything directly on the sheet pan with your hands.

4 cups roughly torn (1-inch) bread pieces (any kind, including crusts)

¼ teaspoon garlic powder

½ teaspoon kosher salt

Up to ⅓ cup extra-virgin olive oil

Preheat the oven to 400°F. Line a sheet pan with foil.

In a large bowl, toss the bread pieces with the garlic powder and salt. Drizzle in just enough olive oil to coat the bread, not drench it. (This will be somewhere between ¼ and ⅓ cup, depending on what kind of bread you use.)

Spread the croutons out on the prepared sheet pan and bake until crunchy and golden, 10 to 12 minutes. Let cool before using.

**Makes 4 cups**

USE IN

CHICKPEA CAESAR SALAD (PAGE 69)

CHILLED ASPARAGUS SOUP WITH
CROUTONS & CHIVES (PAGE 74)

EASIEST WHITE BEAN SOUP (PAGE 78,
SWAPPED IN FOR "GIGANTIC CROUTONS")

TOSSED INTO ANY GREEN SALAD

*Store in an airtight container for
up to 2 weeks.*

the vegetarian's very special bag of hooks & tricks

# Sweet, Creamy Polenta

Here is comfort food at its finest. I usually add the corn kernels only if they are fresh and in-season. If you are feeling indulgent, you can stir in ⅓ cup of cheese (Parmesan, feta, or cheddar all work) along with the butter at the end. To make this vegan, use plant-based butter (and obviously skip the cheese).

**4 cups vegetable stock, store-bought or homemade (page 232)**

**1 teaspoon kosher salt**

**1 cup fine yellow cornmeal**

**Kernels from 1 medium fresh ear of corn (optional)**

**2 tablespoons unsalted butter**

In a medium pot, bring the stock and salt to a boil, then reduce to a simmer over low heat. Add the cornmeal in a slow, steady stream, whisking continuously so it doesn't clump. Continue to stir until the polenta starts pulling away from the sides of the pan, 10 to 12 minutes. Toss in the corn kernels (if using) and the butter and stir until the butter is melted and the corn warmed through, another 1 minute. Let sit, uncovered, for about 5 minutes to allow the polenta to thicken before serving.

### Serves 4 as a side

*USE IN*

*CIDER-BRAISED CABBAGE WEDGES WITH POLENTA (PAGE 59)*

*GLAZED MAITAKE MUSHROOMS WITH SWEET CORN POLENTA (PAGE 56)*

*TOP WITH A SEVEN-MINUTE EGG (PAGE 197)*

**THE CORN STOCK UPGRADE**

*If you replace the vegetable stock with corn stock in your polenta, it will taste almost like corn pudding. To make corn stock, place however many husked ears you have in a stockpot or large pot. Add ½ medium yellow onion (peeled, chopped into two or three large chunks) and a dried bay leaf. Cover with water by an inch and simmer for 1 to 2 hours until the liquid looks brownish gold. If not using right away, divide the stock into resealable freezer bags and freeze them flat on a sheet pan until solid, then stack the bags in the freezer for up to 3 months. Thaw under hot running water or let thaw in the refrigerator overnight.*

# PANTRY STAPLES

# Pickled Onions

When you have pickled onions in your fridge, you'll find that you end up using them on everything—bowls, salads, and sandwiches—where they lend both an acidic brightness in flavor and a visual brightness in color. I find pickling in red or white wine vinegar yields onions that can be used most universally, but I encourage you to experiment with different varieties of vinegar, like unseasoned rice vinegar, apple cider vinegar, and pure white distilled vinegar.

**¼ cup red wine vinegar or white wine vinegar**

**2 tablespoons sugar**

**1 teaspoon kosher salt**

**1 small to medium red onion, halved lengthwise and thinly sliced crosswise**

In a medium heavy saucepan, bring 2 cups water, the vinegar, sugar, and salt to a boil over high heat. When the sugar has dissolved, add the onion slices, reduce the heat to low, and simmer, uncovered, until they have wilted, about 4 minutes. Remove the pan from the heat and set aside to cool to room temp. You can use immediately and store leftovers in their pickling liquid.

Makes 1 cup

*USE IN*

BARLEY BOWLS WITH CHICKPEAS, ROASTED VEGETABLES & AVOCADO DRESSING (PAGE 49)

TACOS WITH REFRIED PINTOS, CRISPY SHIITAKES & KALE (PAGE 102)

STRAIGHT OUT OF THE JAR

ON TOP OF THE COBB SALAD PIZZA (PAGE 40)

*Store onions in their pickling liquid, covered, for up to 2 weeks.*

# Vegetable Stock, Two Ways

Making your own stock sounds high-maintenance, but trust me, even the most novice cook can do it. It requires nothing by way of attention to detail. You can shove almost any vegetable (except bitter vegetables like kale, broccoli. and Brussels sprouts) into a pot, cover it with water, and forget about it for a while. In this way, it's the ideal project for a meditative Sunday afternoon. Once I took on the weekday vegetarian challenge and realized how much stock I was using, I experimented with upgrading it by roasting the vegetables first. If you have time, it definitely makes a difference. The browning adds depth and makes it taste more like chicken stock. Also crucial to depth: mushrooms. Make sure they're in the pot.

the vegetarian's very special bag of hooks & tricks

2 small yellow onions, quartered

4 to 6 ounces mushrooms (any kind: cremini, white, etc., including stems), cleaned and roughly chopped

2 large carrots

4 small celery stalks, with leaves

1 red bell pepper, quartered and seeded

About 4 cups of other roughly chopped vegetables that are lying around, such as leeks, corn cobs, scallions, and zucchini

Extra-virgin olive oil

Kosher salt and freshly ground black pepper to taste

1 tablespoon porcini mushroom powder (optional)

3 medium garlic cloves, peeled and smashed slightly

Handful of fresh thyme or flat-leaf parsley sprigs

**ROASTED VERSION:** Preheat the oven to 400°F. Line a sheet pan with foil.

Toss the onions, mushrooms, carrots, celery, bell pepper, and other mixed vegetables in a large bowl with enough olive oil to coat (not drench), salt, pepper, and the mushroom powder (if using). Lay out flat on the prepared baking sheet. Wrap the garlic cloves in foil and set them on the sheet pan. Roast until the vegetables are golden brown and a little shriveled, 30 to 40 minutes, stirring halfway through.

Transfer the vegetables and garlic into a large stockpot along with a little more salt and pepper, and the thyme or parsley. Add enough water to cover by an inch, bring to a boil over high heat, reduce the heat to a gentle simmer over low heat, and cook for a minimum of 1 hour, preferably between 2 and 3 hours, until the color darkens and the stock tastes rich. You will have to add a little water every now and then to keep the liquid level above the vegetables. Turn off the heat and allow the stock to cool slightly.

Pour the stock through a fine-mesh strainer set over a large bowl. Discard the solids and use the stock, or divide it among small BPA-free, zip-top bags. Seal and freeze them flat on a sheet pan; once frozen, stack the bags in the freezer.

**STOVETOP VERSION:** Break up the quartered onion into large pieces. Combine the mushrooms, onion, and mushroom powder (if using) in 3 tablespoons of olive oil in a large stockpot set over medium-high heat. Cook until the mushrooms have released a little liquid and have started to brown, about 5 minutes. Add the remaining vegetables, salt, pepper, garlic, and thyme. Cover with water by an inch and bring to a boil over high heat, then reduce the heat and simmer on low heat for a minimum of 1 hour, preferably between 2 and 3 hours, until the color darkens and the stock tastes rich. You will have to add a little water every now and then to keep the liquid level above the vegetables. Turn off the heat, allow the stock to cool slightly, and pour it through a fine-mesh strainer set over a large bowl. Discard the solids and use the stock right away, or freeze it in small BPA-free, zip-top bags for up to 3 months.

Makes 4 to 6 cups

USE IN

EASIEST WHITE BEAN SOUP (PAGE 78)

BUTTERNUT SQUASH SOUP WITH
COCONUT MILK & LIME (PAGE 81)

A FARROTTO FOR ALL SEASONS (PAGE 50)

/ vegan /

# Get to Know Your New Best Friends

## Bean Yields

- 1 (15-ounce) can beans = 1½ cups beans
- 1 pound dried beans = 6 to 7 cups cooked
- 1 pound dried lentils = 6 to 7 cups cooked

## Grain Prep

### BARLEY (PEARLED)

*Liquid-to-Grain Ratio:* 3:1

*Yield:* 1 cup uncooked = 3 cups cooked

*Prep:* In a medium pot, combine 1 cup pearled barley and 3 cups water. Bring to a boil, then lower the heat to the laziest simmer, cover, and cook. Check for doneness after 30 minutes. You want the grains to be tripled in size and tender but not mushy. If there is still water left in the pot when they've reached this point—keeping in mind you might have to let them cook another 5 to 10 minutes in a recipe—you can strain the barley in a colander, like pasta.

### FARRO

*Yield:* 1 cup uncooked = 3 cups cooked

*Prep:* Farro cook times can vary wildly depending on a few factors. Pearled farro (where the outer hull has been removed) takes the least time, usually between 20 and 25 minutes, whereas whole farro can take anywhere from 45 to 50 minutes. (This is the kind

you should use for A Farrotto for All Seasons, page 50, where the farro is prepared like risotto.) Another wild card: freshness. If your farro has been sitting on a supermarket shelf for a while, that could affect its cook time. A foolproof way to prepare farro is like pasta—cover it with your cooking liquid (stock or water) and simmer until the grains are chewy-tender but not mushy. Start tasting after 20 minutes, keeping in mind it could take up to 50 minutes. Drain like pasta once it reaches the desired consistency.

### QUINOA

*Liquid-to-Grain Ratio:* 2:1

*Yield:* 1 cup uncooked = 4 cups cooked

*Prep:* Rinse and drain the quinoa in a colander. In a medium pot, bring your water or stock to a boil. Add the quinoa, stir, and cover with a tight-fitting lid. Reduce the heat as low as possible and cook until all of the water has been absorbed, 13 to 15 minutes. Uncover and fluff with a fork.

### WHEAT BERRIES

*Yield:* 1 cup uncooked = 3 cups cooked

*Prep:* I use the same method for wheat berries that I do for farro, that is, I prepare them like pasta. Place the wheat berries in a pot, covering them with water by an inch. Add a pinch of kosher salt and simmer until the grains

CRUSHING IT,
AS USUAL

are tender and the hulls have just started to split open. The cook time will vary (again, based on freshness of the wheat berries)—it can take up to 1 hour for the grains to become tender. Start checking after 45 minutes. Drain the cooked wheat berries in a colander.

## Tofu Prep

### HOW TO PRESS TOFU

You can invest in an actual tofu presser, or you can do what has worked perfectly for me: Slice the tofu block as your recipe instructs. Line a large dinner plate with two paper towels and place the tofu on top. Cover with two more paper towels, then set a cast-iron skillet on top. Let sit for 30 minutes.

### WHEN TO PRESS TOFU

There is no need to press your tofu if a recipe calls for marinating (as in Crispy Smoky Tofu Sandwiches, page 110). It's a good idea to press tofu when you are pan-frying or baking—the more moisture you can expel from the tofu, the crispier it will get.

### HOW TO SLICE TOFU

The tofu I use most often in this book and in my life is the 14- to 15-ounce block of extra-firm that you can usually find in the produce or dairy section of most supermarkets. Though the size of the blocks varies slightly by brand, you can count on them measuring roughly 4½ inches long × 4 inches wide × a little under 2 inches high. Here are the four most common ways I slice those blocks to get them ready for cooking.

*Cubes:* Slice the longest side (4½ inches) of the tofu into 4 even pieces. Rotate the block and do the same with the 4-inch side of the tofu. Slice it into thirds across the middle. You'll have 48 roughly 1-inch cubes.

*Cards:* Slice the longest side (4½ inches) of the tofu into 8 even pieces, each about ¾ inch thick. You'll have eight 4 × 2 × ½-inch pieces.

*Batons:* Follow the instructions for the cards (above), then cut each in half to make sixteen 2 × 2 × ¾-inch pieces.

*Patties:* This is more complicated than the others because if you slice 4 of the ideal-size patties (approximately 3 × 4 × ½ inches, which will fit on a typical sandwich bun, like for Crispy Smoky Tofu Sandwiches, page 110), there will be extra tofu that doesn't lend itself to a patty shape. You can store that extra tofu (in its package with fresh water) for up to another 3 days and use it as desired.

## How to Crush Pistachios, Hazelnuts, and Other Nuts

I like a mix of chunky and almost powdery nuts: Place the nuts in a BPA-free, zip-top bag, sealing it almost entirely. (If you seal it completely, it will burst open when you roll or crush it.) Using a rolling pin or the bottom of a heavy saucepan, pound and press the nuts until half of them look almost powdery and the other half are broken and chunky.

# mix-&-match meal chart

A USE-WHAT-YOU-HAVE FORMULA FOR HOW TO COME UP WITH TONIGHT'S DINNER

**THERE'S AN OLD JOKE I ONCE READ THAT SAID** all the dishes in the world can be traced back to eleven recipes. The thing is, my weeknight self feels like this is actually true. As you can see from the way this book is organized, almost everything I make when I'm on the clock is in the format of a pizza, bowl, taco, pasta, salad, sandwich, or soup—all vehicles for dishes I know my family will like and that I can make without referring to a recipe. Using this logic, I thought I'd leave you with a visual strategy for thinking about dinner combinations that go beyond the hundred-plus recipes you've just flipped through. Got a beautiful butternut squash? Go down the left side of the chart under its column and see if you can come up with a recipe that I haven't given you in this book. (How about . . . pizza with butternut squash and . . . ricotta and thyme? Under "Sandwich," how about smashed roasted butternut squash with basil and aged balsamic on toasted peasant bread? See how easy!) If you can't figure out an idea right away, don't worry; you'll see that many of the recipes in this book are plugged into the chart to help you out. (Along with some helpful prompts; look for "How 'bout?") At the very least, for those of you who have anchored a meal around, say, a chicken breast for most of your life (hello, me) this just might get you thinking about dinner with a whole new strategy. Namely, vegetables first.

| | EGGS | TOFU | BEANS | MUSHROOMS | EGGPLANT | BOK CHOY | BRUSSELS | AVOCADO |
|---|---|---|---|---|---|---|---|---|
| **BOWLS** | Black Rice Bowls with Omelet Ribbons & Snow Peas, page 44 | Rice with Spicy Tofu Crumbles (page 60) | Three-Bean Chili Bowls with Chocolate & Plantain Chips, page 46 | Glazed Maitake Mushrooms with Sweet Corn Polenta, page 56 | Eggplant & Tofu with Sweet-Hot Chili Glaze, page 55 | *how 'bout:* brown rice with roasted or sautéed bok choy, Seven-Minute Egg (page 197) & Teriyaki Sauce (page 211) | Quinoa with Roasted Winter Vegetables, page 61 | *how 'bout:* avocado & Brussels sprouts bowls on coconutty rice |
| | *how 'bout:* breakfast burrito bowls | Eggplant & Tofu with Sweet-Hot Chili Glaze, page 55 | Coconut Curried Red Lentils, page 162 | A Farrotto for All Seasons (page 50) with mushrooms & asparagus | | | A Farrotto for All Seasons (page 50) with Brussels sprouts & peas | |
| | | | Spicy-Tangy-Smoky Pinto Bean Bowls, page 52 | *how 'bout:* farro bowls with garlicky mushrooms, parm, & parsley | | | Barley Bowls with Chickpeas, Roasted Vegetables & Avocado Dressing, page 49 | |
| **PIZZAS** | Pizza with Cheddar, Caramelized Onion & Egg, page 34 | | | *how 'bout:* white pizza topped with assorted mushrooms | *how 'bout:* cheese pizza topped with breaded eggplant | | | *how 'bout:* pizza with smoked mozzarella & shredded Brussels sprouts |
| **SALADS** | Chickpea Caesar Salad, page 69 | Wheat Berries with Crispy Tofu, Grapes, Arugula & Feta, page 62 | Pizza Salad with White Beans, page 66 | | | | | *how 'bout:* avocado-black bean salad with red onion, cilantro & All-Purpose Vinaigrette, page 217 |
| | | Cabbage-Kale-Tofu Salad with Citrusy Ginger Dressing, page 65 | Chickpea Caesar Salad, page 69 | | | | | |
| | | | Strawberry-Feta Salad with Beets & Beans, page 70 | | | | | |
| | | | Pizza Salad with White Beans, page 66 | | | | | |
| **TOASTS / SANDWICHES** | *how 'bout:* NY deli–style egg sandwich with American cheese and hot sauce | Tofu Bánh Mì, page 113 | Veggie Burgers, page 120 | Veggie Burger, page 120 | *how 'bout:* eggplant parm sandwiches! | | | Coconutty Avocado Toasts, page 187 |
| | | Crispy Smoky Tofu Sandwiches, page 110 | | *how 'bout:* sautéed mixed mushrooms & greens on Gruyère toasts | | | | |

| ARTICHOKE | KALE | TOMATOES | SQUASH | CAULIFLOWER | ASPARAGUS | BEETS | POTATOES | MISC |
|---|---|---|---|---|---|---|---|---|
| | *how 'bout:* wheat berries with kale, feta, sliced almonds & pomegranate seeds | A Farrotto for All Seasons (page 50) with Corn & Tomatoes | A Farrotto for All Seasons (page 50) with Butternut Squash & Crispy Sage | *how 'bout:* roasted fried cauliflower (with chili flakes and parm) on quinoa with a Seven-Minute Egg, page 197 | A Farrotto for All Seasons (page 50) with Mushrooms & Asparagus | *how 'bout:* farro with beets, dill & feta | | Cider-Braised Cabbage Wedges with Polenta, page 59 |
| | | | | | | | | Quinoa with Roasted Winter Vegetables, page 61 |
| | | | | | | | | |
| Artichoke Dip Pizza, page 37 | | | Zucchini Pizza, page 38 | *how 'bout:* pizza with roasted cauliflower, tomatoes & olives | | | *how 'bout:* pizza with paper-thin slices of potatoes, cheddar & thyme or rosemary | Cobb Salad Pizza, page 40 |
| | Our Favorite Kale Salad with Almonds & Dried Cranberries, page 174 | Tomato-Nectarine Salad, page 186 | *how 'bout:* arugula salad with roasted butternut squash, lentils, feta & candied walnuts or pecans | | | Strawberry-Feta Salad with Beets & Beans, page 70 | | |
| | | Tomato Salad with Avocado-Basil Dressing, page 186 | | | | | | Chopped Broccolini Salad with Dill & Feta, page 173 |
| | | | | | | | | |
| | | *how 'bout:* classic heirloom tomato sandwiches | | | *how 'bout:* ricotta toasts with asparagus & chili oil | | | |
| | | | | | *how 'bout:* asparagus tart on puff pastry | | | |

| | EGGS | TOFU | BEANS | MUSHROOMS | EGGPLANT | BOK CHOY | BRUSSELS | AVOCADO |
|---|---|---|---|---|---|---|---|---|
| **PIES/DUMPLINGS** | | | | | | | | |
| | Quiche #1: Sweet Onion, Spinach & Cheddar, page 115 | *how 'bout*: dumplings stuffed with tofu, kale, ginger & garlic | | Mushroom-Leek Galette, page 123 | | | | |
| **SKILLETS** | | | | | | | | |
| | Crispy Cabbage Pancakes, page 132 | Teriyaki-Glazed Crispy Tofu with Green Beans, page 135 | Spicy Chickpeas with Tomatoes & Greens, page 139 | Mushroom–Bok Choy Packed Fried Rice, page 136 | | Mushroom–Bok Choy Packed Fried Rice, page 136 | | |
| | *how 'bout*: frittatas | Tofu with Broccoli & Spicy Peanut Sauce, page 133 | Crispy Chickpeas with Naan & Yogurt Sauce, page 140 | | | | | |
| | | | Crunchy-Cheesy Bean Bake, page 143 | | | | | |
| **PASTAS** | | | | | | | | |
| | *how 'bout*: bacon-less spaghetti carbonara | *how 'bout*: Tofu Bánh Mì–Style Soba Noodles, page 114 | | *how 'bout*: fettuccini with sautéed mushrooms & parmesan | *how 'bout*: rigatoni with garlicky roasted eggplant & tomato sauce, bocconcini & parm | *how 'bout*: soba noodles with crispy roasted bok choy tossed with sesame-soy-garlic dressing | *how 'bout*: orrechiette with sautéed shredded Brussels sprouts & caramelized onions | |
| **TACOS/TORTILLAS ETC** | | | | | | | | |
| | Migas Tacos, page 97 | Tacos with Spicy Tofu Crumbles (page 60) & fixins | Refried Black Bean Tostadas with Avocado & Pickled Onions, page 98 | Tacos with Refried Pintos, Crispy Shiitakes, & Kale, page 102 | | | *you try now*: What tacos would you make with Brussels sprouts? | Refried Black Bean Tostadas with Avocado & Pickled Onions, page 98 |
| | | | Roasted Butternut Squash & Black Bean Tacos, page 101 | | | | | |
| | | | Andy's Sunday Enchiladas with Red Sauce, page 106 | | | | | |
| | | | Green Enchiladas with Tomatillo Sauce, page 105 | | | | | |
| | | | Tacos with Refried Pintos, Crispy Shiitakes, & Kale, page 102 | | | | | |

| ARTICHOKE | KALE | TOMATOES | SQUASH | CAULIFLOWER | ASPARAGUS | BEETS | POTATOES | MISC |
|---|---|---|---|---|---|---|---|---|
| Quiche #2: Artichoke-Parm, page 116 | | *how 'bout:* tomato tart on puff pastry | | | | | *how 'bout:* samosas with peas, potatoes, & tamarind sauce | |
| | Spicy Chickpeas with Tomatoes & Greens, page 139 | | | Spicy Cauliflower Fritters with Pea Shoots, page 129 | | | *how 'bout:* frittatas | |
| | | | | Cauliflower Cutlets with Romesco Sauce, page 144 | | | | |
| | | | | | | | | |
| *you try now:* What pasta would you make with artichokes? | The Greenest Pasta (Spaghetti with Peas, Broccolini & Kale Pesto), page 92 | Tagliatelle with Corn, Tomatoes, "Onion-Bacon" & Basil, page 87 | Rigatoni with Honeynut Squash, Chard & Hazelnuts, page 84 | | | | | Chickpea-Pasta Mac & Cheese with Chopped Tomatoes, page 88 |
| | | *how 'bout:* pasta with fresh tomato & basil sauce | | | | | | The Greenest Pasta (Spaghetti with Peas, Broccolini & Kale Pesto), page 92 |
| | Tacos with Refried Pintos, Crispy Shiitakes & Kale, page 102 | | Roasted Butternut Squash & Black Bean Tacos, page 101 | *how 'bout:* tacos stuffed with crispy cauliflower florets, chickpeas, lime & capers | *how 'bout:* asparagus & goat cheese quesadillas | | | |

| EGGS | TOFU | BEANS | MUSHROOMS | EGGPLANT | BOK CHOY | BRUSSELS | AVOCADO |
|---|---|---|---|---|---|---|---|
| **SOUPS** | | | | | | | |
| *how 'bout:* avgolemono (made with Vegetable Stock, page 232) and orzo | *how 'bout:* miso soup with tofu & spinach | Easiest White Bean Soup, page 78 | *how 'bout:* cream of mushroom soup | | *how 'bout:* miso soup with tofu & bok choy | | *how 'bout:* chilled cucumber-avocado-yogurt soup |
| | | Stewy Black Lentils with Chard & Feta, page 77 | | | | | |
| **SMALL PLATES** | | | | | | | |
| *how 'bout:* deviled eggs topped with herbs, capers & minced red onions | | Herby, Brothy Lima Beans, page 160 | | Roasted Eggplant & Tomatoes with Miso-Tahini Sauce, page 178 | Sesame Bok Choy, page 184 | Hot Honey Brussels Sprouts (page 172) on a bed of The Creamiest Hummus (page 164) | Peppery Sprout Salad with Avocado, page 170 |
| | | Marinated Beans, page 163 | | *how 'bout:* roasted or breaded-fried eggplant on a bed of The Creamiest Hummus (page 164) with feta, mint & chili oil | | | |
| | | | | *how 'bout:* baba ghanoush | | | |

| ARTICHOKE | KALE | TOMATOES | SQUASH | CAULIFLOWER | ASPARAGUS | BEETS | POTATOES | MISC |
|---|---|---|---|---|---|---|---|---|
| | | | Butternut Squash Soup with Coconut Milk & Lime, page 81 | how 'bout: cream of cauliflower soup with Hand-Torn Croutons (page 226) and rosemary | Chilled Asparagus Soup with Croutons & Chives, page 74 | | how 'bout: cold potato soup with chives | |
| | | | | | | | how 'bout: warm potato soup with chives | |
| how 'bout: artichoke hearts with parsleyed butter | Steamed Kale with Spicy Peanut Sauce, page 172 | how 'bout: sliced tomatoes with feta & parsley | Roasted Honeynut Squash with Crispy Sage Leaves, page 188 | how 'bout: roasted crispy cauliflower tossed with toasted pine nuts, raisins, parsley & vinaigrette (such as All-Purpose Vinaigrette, page 217) | how 'bout: warm asparagus salad with chopped egg & red onion | Roasted Beets with Quick-Pickled Cabbage & Dill, page 171 | Greek-Style Lemon-Oregano Potatoes, page 180 | Slivered Minty Sugar Snap Peas on a Bed of Ricotta, page 174 |
| how 'bout: giving artichokes the eggplant parm treatment | | | | | | Roasted Beets with Herby Yogurt & Pistachios, page 176 | Andy's Spicy Diced Potatoes, page 182 | Brown Butter Corn with Parsley, page 184 |
| | | | | | | Pink Hummus, page 164 | Restuffed Japanese Sweet Potatoes with Miso & Chives, page 190 | Dill Slaw, page 187 |
| | | | | | | | | Any-Which-Way Chopped, Charred Broccolini, page 173 |

# acknowledgments

People ask me all the time how I come up with my recipe ideas. You'd think that after writing about food for fifteen years (including five cookbooks) that I'd have a pretty good answer by now. The truth is, recipe-generating is far from a straightforward or solo process, and to suggest otherwise is misleading. Much as I'd love to tell you that I was brought up cooking at the apron hems of my Italian nonna and Jewish bubbie, I wasn't. In fact, I never knew any of my grandparents (they all died before I was born), let alone whether they preferred fennel in their meatballs or onions in their latkes. Like a lot of modern home cooks, I learned how to cook and create an arsenal of go-to family recipes from what I'd call enthusiastic trial and error, by discovering recipes in magazines and on websites and, especially, following trusted voices in the proverbial "village." In my case, that village includes my mom, who put a homemade dinner on the table every night in spite of working full-time, and who, in spite of her 100 percent Italian heritage, appreciated the power of a shortcut. And my husband, who threatens to divorce me if I don't generously salt the water when I'm making pasta. And my mother-in-law, Emily, who mailed me a pack of family recipes handwritten on index cards when I joined the family. And Aunt Patty, who first introduced me to Marcella Hazan. It includes Marcella Hazan herself, of course, who taught me more about authentic Italian

cooking than either of my kids' two 100 percent Italian grandmothers. If we're going down that road, it also includes a whole *lot* of cookbook authors, and professional chefs I've never met: It includes David Chang, Madhur Jaffrey, Marcus Samuelsson, and Martha Stewart. And Nigel Slater, Michael Anthony, Alice Waters, Deborah Madison, and Yotam Ottolenghi, the four of whom taught me so much about why certain ingredients go with specific vegetables; and it includes Andrea Nguyen for teaching me a foolproof way to pan-fry tofu. It includes chefs from restaurants I've had the privilege to dine in over the years—from the dim sum spot in the Central District of Hong Kong to the taco truck in Austin with the best migas tacos on earth, to the bougie plant-based DIY salad bar in Brooklyn. It includes Chipotle! And Shake Shack! And Blooming Hill Farm, the rustic, vegetable-forward café in Duchess County, New York, that made me realize how much I loved nuts crushed to powder on my salads! It includes my sister, Lynn, for giving me a subscription to *Gourmet* magazine in 1994. It includes an embarrassing amount of Instagram influencers, including the one who's never met a cheese plate she didn't call EPICCCCC!!!!

Ultimately, my point is this: The recipes in these pages belong to that village as much as they belong to me. I'm just the lucky one who gets to present them to you.

# acknowledgments

This is my fourth cookbook in the *Dinner: A Love Story* series, and I'm always amazed that somehow for each one, I've had the privilege to work with a team of friends and professionals who all seem to care about my project as much as I do. At the top of the list are the magicians at Clarkson Potter: Raquel Pelzel, my editor extraordinaire, whose fingerprints are all over these pages—from the tightly edited recipes to the behind-the-scenes cheerleading you'll have to trust me happened as a matter of course; Stephanie Huntwork, who oversaw the art direction, holding my hand (via Zoom calls) during shoots, indulging my all-over-the-place Pinterest boards and sketches, and ultimately assigning the brilliant, on-the-nose designer Laura Palese to execute that "vision" to perfection. All the behind-the-scenes worker bees who make everything feel consistent and orderly: editorial superstar Bianca Cruz, copyeditor Kathy Brock, indexer Thérèse Shere, and production editor Patricia Shaw. Lastly: Francis Lam, Doris Cooper, and Aaron Wehner, for having faith in the project all the way through.

A huge thank-you to the photography team: First and foremost, Christine Han, whose confidence and demeanor always seemed to communicate "Trust me." (I was always glad I did!) Thank you for making every image look a thousand times better than I could've ever imagined, and for just being so cool and fun to be around. To food stylist Olivia Mack McCool, who made every dish look like its best self, and who somehow ended up doubling (and tripling) as prop and wardrobe stylist. To digital technician Stephanie Munguia, the consummate professional, and to my two indispensable kitchen assistants, Lily Soroka and Marni Blank: I could not have done it without you three! Lastly, a big shout-out to little Coco and Dean for lending me your new moms all day even though you were just barely born. (You can thank me for reminding them to pump all that delicious breast milk for you every two to three hours.)

Speaking of the photo shoot, big-time gratitude for the partners who supplied the props: East Fork Pottery; Revol USA; Melissa Lauprete, the mastermind behind AtLand, maybe the most beautiful shop in the New York area; ceramicist Sarah Donato, who lent me her gorgeous, one-of-a-kind bowls and dishes (please look up her company, Signe Ceramics); and to Anthony Terranova from Terranova Bakery, who keeps my freezer filled with 16-ounce pizza doughs and pane di casa all year long, not just during photo shoot weeks. (I know! How does one get so lucky?)

To Christy Knell, Christina Cohen, and Katherine Bagby for creating HudCo—the coolest, most inspiring workshare collective in Westchester County, NY—so I could have the time and space when I needed it most.

How much do I love and appreciate my network of food-loving friends? It's impossible to measure. Thanks to those of you who have at one time or another (a) texted me something along the lines of "I made your ____ last night, it was so

249

*acknowledgments*

good!" (b) bought any of my books for yourself or as gifts, (c) sent me a link to a very Jenny recipe and saying "This seems like a very Jenny recipe," (d) volunteered to be a real-life official tester, (e) just *been there* to cheer me on, or (f) all of the above. You know who you are: Robin Helman, Jenn Meyer, Ben Gardner, Jodi Levine, Ingrid Katz, Cara Thanassi, Cara Moretti, Clarisa Gracia, Jennie Kotler, Naria Halliwell, Dorian Pascoe, Julie Fischer, Jennifer Polimeno, Sonya Terjanian, Kate Solomon Sonders, Joanna Goddard, Kimberlee Rhodes, Caroline D'Onofrio, Maureen Heffernan, Tom Prince, Todd Lawlor, Anne Scharer, Jodi Levine, Alisa Greenspan, Jeni Goldman Silbert, Rory Evans, Catherine Hong, Bonnie Stelzer, Lori Slater, Liz Egan, Barbara Shornick.

Thank you to the Rosenstrachs (Mom, Dad, Phil, Nathan); the Wards (Emily, Steve, Tony, Trish, Sophia, Aidan, Luca); and the Zerbibs (Nick, Lynn, Alison, Amanda, Owen). Because it feels wrong to do anything food-related without bringing the whole family along.

Lastly, to Andy, Phoebe, and Abby. This is the fourth and (maybe) final book I'll write about the four of us sitting in our red chairs around the kitchen table, eating family dinner. It goes without saying that none of this—the books, the blog, any of the writing—would have been possible without you. And, Phoebe and Abby, though it might seem like I'm the one cooking and taking care of you two all the time, it's really the opposite. Nothing has been more personally meaningful to me than sharing a table with you night after night, watching you grow into smart, engaged, kind citizens of the world who are now off to college. Come back soon! Dinner's at seven.

# index

*index*